Dark Psychology 3 in 1

This book includes:
Dark Psychology Secrets – Speed Reading People - Rewire your Mind.

Benedict Spot - Richard Empath

This Book Includes

Book 1:

Dark Psychology

Manipulation, persuasion techniques, and mind control methods. Learn how to win friends and influence people. A step by step guide.

Book 2:

Speed - Reading People

A step by step guide to understand how to analyze people. Learn body language secrets and the art of manipulate people through this workbook

Book 3:

Rewire Your Mind

Rewire Your Brain to Become a Manipulator. A Workbook to Discover Your Personality and Change Your Mind

© Copyright 2021 - All rights reserved.

Table of Contents

INTRODUCTION 12

Dark Psychology

INTRODUCTION 18

CHAPTER 1: WHAT IS MENTAL MANIPULATION 22

CHAPTER 2: WHAT IS DARK PSYCHOLOGY 24

CHAPTER 3: HISTORICAL OUTLINE OF MENTAL
MANIPULATION... 26

    BRAIN PHASES 27

CHAPTER 4: TECHNIQUES USED IN MENTAL
MANIPULATION... 28

    PERSUASION TECHNIQUE 28
    SUBLIMINAL PROGRAMMING 28

CHAPTER 5: WHAT ARE THE SIGNS OF MANIPULATION AS IT
IS USED IN TODAY IN THE WORLD (PRACTICAL EXAMPLES)
....32

    CHURCHES 32
    FAMILIES 36
    POLITICS..37

CHAPTER 6: HOW TO RECOGNIZE A MANIPULATOR AND
WHAT ARE THE SIGNS OF MANIPULATION (ADD A LOT OF
DETAILS) 40

    MANIPULATORS UNDERMINE YOUR CONVICTION TO GRASP THE REALITY 41
    THEIR ACTIONS AND WORDS ARE DISSIMILAR... 41
    THEY ARE GOOD AT A GUILT-TRIPPING THEIR VICTIMS 41
    THEY HAVE AN APPETITE FOR POWER...42
    DOES HE OR SHE RAISE HIS OR HER VOICE?...42
    THEY USE NEGATIVE JOKES TO HURT YOU 42
    SWEET-TALKING 42
    THEY TAKE ADVANTAGE OF ALL WEAK SPOTS 43
    THEY ALWAYS HAVE IT WORSE THAN YOU DO 43
    THEY USE CHARM AND NICENESS 43
    THEY ARE FOND OF DENYING 44

THEY USE LIES AS A WEAPON 44

GENEROSITY WITH GIFTS 44

THEY USE COMPLIMENTS IN EXCESS 44

FORCED TEAMING 45

SIGNS OF MANIPULATION 45

HOME COURT ADVANTAGE 45

PLAIN OLD BULLYING 45

TUGGING ON YOUR HEARTSTRINGS... 46

EMOTIONAL BLACKMAIL.. 46

PLAYING THE VICTIM... 46

GASLIGHTING 46

CHAPTER 7: HOW TO DEFEND YOURSELF FROM THOSE WHO WANT TO MANIPULATE US 48

IGNORE EVERYTHING THEY DO AND SAY...................................... 49

HIT THEIR CENTER OF GRAVITY.. 50

TRUST THE JUDGMENTS YOU MAKE.. 51

TRY TO FIT IN 52

CHAPTER 8: HYPNOSIS AND SELF-HYPNOSIS 54

IMPROVING DEEP SLEEP 55

IT EASES SYMPTOMS OF IRRITABLE BOWEL SYNDROME. 56

CALMING NERVES 56

TREATMENT OF LIFE-STYLE DISEASES SUCH AS HYPERTENSION 57

MEMORY IMPROVEMENT 57

IMPROVES CONCENTRATION AND FOCUS..................................... 58

CHAPTER 9: EMOTIONAL MANIPULATION (HOW ITS MECHANISM WORKS) 60

OWNING SPACE 61

YOUR WORDS AGAINST YOU 61

GUILT 62

POSITIVE AND NEGATIVE EMOTIONS.. 62

ANGER 63

SELF-DISCIPLINE AND CONFIDENCE 63

SURPRISES 64

CRITICISM... 64

DOUBT 65

IGNORANCE 65

CHAPTER 10: HOW TO LEARN TO USE MANIPULATION TO YOUR ADVANTAGE..**66**

EMOTIONAL INTELLIGENCE 66
CHARMS AND FLIRTS...67
INVEST IN SELF-CONFIDENCE..67
ACT..68
EMPATHY..68
APPRENTICESHIP 69
MIRRORING 69

CHAPTER 11: WHAT COMMUNICATION AND VERBAL SKILLS NEED TO BE DEVELOPED TO IMPROVE PERSUASION AND MANIPULATION SKILLS? **70**

LISTENING SKILLS 71
OPEN COMMUNICATION 71
REINFORCEMENT..72
QUESTIONING...72
REFLECTING AND CLARITY..73
NEGOTIATION SKILLS 73
IMPORTANCE OF DEVELOPING COMMUNICATION AND VERBAL SKILLS IN MANIPULATION 74

CHAPTER 12: HOW TO USE MANIPULATION TO MANIPULATE, PERSUADE AND INFLUENCE PEOPLE..............**76**

FEAR AND RELIEF TECHNIQUE 77
GUILTY APPROACH TECHNIQUE...78
PLAYING THE VICTIM 79
LOVE BOMBING TECHNIQUE 79
BRIBERY TECHNIQUE..80
BECOMING A GOOD LISTENER...80

CHAPTER 13: THE BEST TECHNIQUES OF PERSUASION **82**

MIMICKING 83
SOCIAL PROOF 84
RECIPROCITY...85
CONSISTENCY AND COMMITMENT 86

Speed - Reading People

CHAPTER 1: HOW TO UNDERSTAND IN ADVANCE THE CHARACTER OF A PERSON 92

CHAPTER 2: BODY LANGUAGE; HOW IMPORTANT IS IT AND WHAT CAN WE LEARN? 96

THE ROLE OF BODY LANGUAGE IN COMMUNICATION 97
GIVING CUES 98
CONFLICTING/ WORD AND ACTION DO NOT MATCH. 98
USING IT IN PLACE OF WORDS 98
GIVING MEAT TO WHAT WE SAY/ENHANCING 98
GIVING DIRECTION 99
INFORMATION FROM BODY LANGUAGE 99
INTEREST 99
INTENTION 100
CHARACTER/PERSONALITY 100

CHAPTER 3: KNOW YOURSELF WELL TO UNDERSTAND OTHERS 102

IDENTIFY YOUR PERSONALITY 103
BODY POSTURE 103
BE FLEXIBLE WHEN COMMUNICATING 103
PRACTICE FACIAL EXPRESSION 104
INTENTION 104
GESTURES 104

CHAPTER 4: BODY LANGUAGE: BODY PARTS (THE MOVEMENTS AND POSTURES THAT TRANSMIT MESSAGES) 106

KINESICS 106
BODY POSTURE - CLOSED/OPEN ARMS, SLUMPED SHOULDERS, ETC 107
MIRRORING 107
FACIAL EXPRESSIONS 108
PROXEMICS 109
CLOSE DISTANCE - INTEREST 109
SOCIAL DISTANCE - IMPERSONAL/FORMAL 109
PUBIC DISTANCE - RESPECTABILITY 110

CHAPTER 5: BODY LANGUAGE IN MEN AND WOMEN -WHAT ARE ALL THOSE GESTURES THAT HIDE UNSPOKEN WORDS 112

FACIAL EXPRESSIONS 112
THE EYES 113
THE MOUTH 114
ARMS AND LEGS 115
POSTURE 116
PROXIMITY 116

CHAPTER 6: HOW TO DECIPHER VERBAL COMMUNICATION 118

BE AN ACTIVE LISTENER 118
BE EMPATHETIC 121
SEEK TO UNDERSTAND FIRST 122

CHAPTER 7: THE MEANING OF THE WORDS 124

PITCH 125
PICK CUES 126
LOOK OUT FOR REPETITIONS 127

CHAPTER 8: HOW TO PAY ATTENTION TO DETAILS 130

THE LINK BETWEEN BODY MOVEMENT AND WORDS 130
"WE ARE SADDENED" 132
"BEYOND THE COMPREHENSION OF WORDS" 132
"BROTHERS AND SISTERS" 132
"EFFORT IN FUTILITY" 132
"MURKY" 133
"LOGICAL CONCLUSION" 133

CHAPTER 9: LIES (LIKE DISCOVERING A LIE, THE BEST TECHNIQUE TO UNDERSTAND A LIE FROM MOVEMENTS OF WORDS, OR IN BEHAVIOR) 134

CHAPTER 10: TRUTH (HOW TO RECOGNIZE A FACT) 138

CHAPTER 11: TECHNIQUES AND PRACTICAL METHODS TO ACTIVELY ANALYZE PEOPLE 142

HOW TO ASK THE RIGHT QUESTIONS 143
WHEN TO BE AGGRESSIVE 144
WHEN TO OBSERVE THE BEHAVIOR OF OTHERS 145

CHAPTER 12: HOW TO TAKE ADVANTAGE OF THE
TECHNIQUES LEARNED TO ACHIEVE SUCCESS AND ENJOY
THE ESTEEM OF OTHERS..146

KNOWING YOURSELF 146
TRUTH 147
INTERPRETING PERSONALITY...148

BOOK 2: "DARK PSYCHOLOGY: REWIRE YOUR MIND
WORKBOOK"..150

CHAPTER 13: APPLYING MANIPULATION AND MIND
REPROGRAMMING IN DIFFERENT ROLES 152

SALESPERSON 152
MANAGER DEALING WITH STAFF 155
AN EMPLOYEE DEALING WITH A NEGATIVE BOSS 158
LONER 160
ENTREPRENEUR..163
ROMANTIC RELATIONSHIP 165
GROUP LEADER 167
PARENT..169
MARKETER 172
STUDENT 174
POLITICIAN 177

Rewire Your Mind

CHAPTER 1: IMPORTANCE OF MINDSET 184

SUCCESS VS. FAILURE 184

CHAPTER 2: ALL ABOUT THE MIND 190

MIND VS. BRAIN 190
THE CONSCIOUS AND THE UNCONSCIOUS MIND 194

CHAPTER 3: THOUGHTS AND ACTIONS 198

LINK BETWEEN THOUGHTS, DECISIONS, ACTIONS, AND RESULTS............198

CHAPTER 4: PARADIGM IS IMPORTANT 204

WHAT IS A PARADIGM?.. 204
HOW TO CHANGE YOUR PARADIGM? 205
WHY REPROGRAM YOUR MIND?.. 208

CHAPTER 5: MANIPULATION IS NOT BAD 214

MANIPULATION IS DESIRABLE 214
SELF-AWARENESS IS THE FIRST STEP 217

CHAPTER 6: REWIRING THE MIND 224

THE LAW OF ATTRACTION 224
WHAT IS A NEGATIVE PARADIGM? 227
HOW TO RECOGNIZE NEGATIVE PATTERNS 228
PATTERNS TO AVOID 230
HOW TO REPLACE NEGATIVE PATTERNS....................................233
SKILLS FOR MANIPULATION 238
IMPORTANCE OF VISUALIZATION AND REPETITION 240

Introduction

E very time dark psychology comes up, we always think of mind control, persuasion, and manipulation. Generally speaking, we tend to believe that some evil art is practiced for the sake of advancing some malicious agenda. Other times, most individuals believe that we are talking about some type of magic spells that are cast on the minds of people.

The fact of the matter that dark psychology derives its name from the fact that it deals with the ways in which individuals, organizations and even governments can use mental triggers to sway people's opinions one way or another.

For instance, governments tend to highly publicize their achievements in order to convince voters that they are doing a good job. This is quite common when incumbents are up to for reelection or are looking to further their foothold.

Skeptics like to point out how religions and advertisers use dark psychology, through mental manipulation, to essentially brainwash people to go along with their agendas. The fact is that "brainwashing" as is generally portrayed in Hollywood films that quite work that way.

That is, when you think about manipulation, it isn't about a group of thugs beating people and force-feeding them content so that victims and easily controllable.

In reality, mental manipulation is a very subtle art. When done properly, subjects don't even know they are being manipulated. As a matter of fact, they are perfectly happy to go along with the manipulators' agenda.

Consider this example: Advertisers often use scare tactics to persuade you to purchase an item. They will generally present you with a problem, which is usually life-altering (though it generally isn't), and then with a solution. The solution is the product or service which they sell. Then, they load up on the consequences that come with not acquiring their solution. So, if you don't buy their product, you will suffer grave consequences.

A common example is health. A great deal of products in the health industry are aimed at weight loss. So, advertisers claim that if you are overweight you are prone to any number of health risks.

While the science backs that up, they blow those claims out of proportion. This leads folks to begin to question their health. Then, the advertiser will present their product as the ultimate weight-loss solution. Finally, you will be a healthy individual because you have lost weight thanks to their product.

While all of that may actually be true, some advertisers go over the top by including bogus science, false testimonials and actors posing as doctors.

Some of the more gullible viewers fall for the advertising and purchase the product(s). The products' ultimate effectiveness is then up to the user's own experience.

In this book, we will be taking a look at how you can learn how dark psychology works so that you can not only recognize when such techniques are being used on you, but how you can read people as well.

This will help you vastly improve your personal relationships while helping you get ahead in all facets of your life. So, whether you are brand new to this subject or whether you have learned about it in the past, this volume will certainly provide you with fresh insights and perspective on how dark psychology is used in everyday life.

Dark Psychology

Manipulation, persuasion techniques, and mind control methods. Learn how to win friends and influence people. A step by step guide.

Benedict Spot

Introduction

Every time dark psychology comes up, we always think of mind control, persuasion, and manipulation. Generally speaking, we tend to believe that some evil art is practiced for the sake of advancing some malicious agenda. Other times, most individuals believe that we are talking about some type of magic spells that are cast on the minds of people.

The fact of the matter that dark psychology derives its name from the fact that it deals with the ways in which individuals, organizations and even governments can use mental triggers to sway people's opinions one way or another.

For instance, governments tend to highly publicize their achievements in order to convince voters that they are doing a good job. This is quite common when incumbents are up to for reelection or are looking to further their foothold.

Skeptics like to point out how religions and advertisers use dark psychology, through mental manipulation, to essentially brainwash people to go along with their agendas. The fact is that "brainwashing" as is generally portrayed in Hollywood films that quite work that way. That is, when you think about manipulation, it isn't about a group of thugs beating people and force-feeding them content so that victims and easily controllable.

In reality, mental manipulation is a very subtle art. When done properly, subjects don't even know they are being manipulated. As a matter of fact, they are perfectly happy to go along with the manipulators' agenda.

Consider this example: Advertisers often use scare tactics to persuade you to purchase an item.

They will generally present you with a problem, which is usually life-altering (though it generally isn't), and then with a solution. The solution is the product or service which they sell.

Then, they load up on the consequences that come with not acquiring their solution. So, if you don't buy their product, you will suffer grave consequences.

A common example is health. A great deal of products in the health industry are aimed at weight loss. So, advertisers claim that if you are overweight you are prone to any number of health risks.

While the science backs that up, they blow those claims out of proportion. This leads folks to begin to question their health. Then, the advertiser will present their product as the ultimate weight-loss solution. Finally, you will be a healthy individual because you have lost weight thanks to their product.

While all of that may actually be true, some advertisers go over the top by including bogus science, false testimonials and actors posing as doctors. Some of the more gullible viewers fall for the advertising and purchase the product(s). The products' ultimate effectiveness is then up to the user's own experience.

In this book, we will be taking a look at how you can learn how dark psychology works so that you can not only recognize when such techniques are being used on you, but how you can read people as well.

This will help you vastly improve your personal relationships while helping you get ahead in all facets of your life. So, whether you are brand new to this subject or whether you have learned about it in the past, this volume will certainly provide you with fresh insights and perspective on how dark psychology is used in everyday life.

CHAPTER 1:

What Is Mental Manipulation

The term "mental manipulation" is often thrown around on social media and in mainstream communications. In fact, it is quite common to hear this expression used in reference to large public events, political campaigning and advertising. The fact of the matter is that most folks have a general understanding of what it refers to but may not be clear on the specific of what this term encompasses.

In short, mental manipulation is controlling and twisting a person's state of mind to make them want to do what you want to be done. A manipulator influences the will of others through the use deception or underhand techniques.

As such, manipulation implies a degree of force upon targets, that is, the manipulator will try their best to force their targets to do what they will, especially if the targets do not wish to comply.

Now, I am not talking about kidnapping folks and brainwashing them like it is done in the movies. I am talking about subtle techniques and strategies which are used to get others to go along without them actually realizing they are being manipulated.

As a matter of fact, the best manipulators make it seem like people are doing things of their own accord rather than acting upon the provocation of some external force. Nevertheless, there is a degree of forces that goes along with manipulation. For example, television stations will force you to watch their programming and advertising in order to get you to purchase the products and services of their sponsor's.

However, the coercion shown in this case is quite simple to get around: you can just change the channel. Yet, programming and advertising is designed in such a way that you won't want to change channel.

Other types of manipulation can be a lot more overt. For instance, political parties and candidates will promote themselves by littering their campaigns with calls to action such as "vote for the best candidate" or "vote for so-and-so if you value your children's future". These calls to action are blatant attempts at swaying voters' opinions.

That is why the first part of this book is dedicated to understanding and identifying manipulation as it is commonly practiced. I am not talking about some dark cabal that is trying to secretly rule the world through controlling the minds of every single human on this planet. In fact, I am referring to the ways in which trained individuals will attempt to influence your opinion to get you to go along with their agenda.

When you uncover their techniques, you will not only be able to protect yourself, and your loved ones, from these influences, you will be also be able to get your own agenda across. While I am not asking you to openly go out there and control the minds of those with whom you come into contact, I am asking you to use these techniques to help you get ahead when you need that extra nudge.

So, sit back because we are going on quite a ride.

CHAPTER 2:

What Is Dark Psychology

Dark psychology is the art of using manipulation and mind control over others. It is the study of human conditions about how people prey on others. We all have the potential to oppress other human beings and creatures. Most of us restrain this feeling, but some utilize it. Dark psychology tries to find out the perceptions, behaviors, and thoughts that lead to this preying behavior. In most cases, dark psychology has found that 99.99% is goal-oriented, and the remaining 0.01% manipulate others with no purpose and with no influence from religious dogma and science. Therefore, dark psychology is the trend in which people use techniques like persuasion, manipulation, and motivation to get their way. What is a dark psychology triad?

Dark psychology triad is the seeking to foretell the criminal behavior and manipulation in relationships. These triads are narcissism, which is the grandiosity, egotism, and lacking empathy, psychopathy, which is using charm and friendliness, but lacking empathy, selfishness, and remorsefulness to get what you want and Machiavellianism, which is manipulating others with deception and lacking morality in your manipulation. Nobody wants to be manipulated, but in today's world, we are prone to be manipulated. It does not have to be in extreme cases like the dark triad above, but we are manipulated in simple actions that may seem harmless and normal. You will find this manipulation in sales techniques, in the internet ads, and our children when they seek to get what they want. People we love and trust a lot apply dark psychology to us.

Dark psychology involves everything that human beings are in their dark part. We all have a masked side within us from birth that is evil. Dark psychology has found out that these people who do these acts never do it for sex, power, retribution, or any other purpose. They commit these heinous acts with no goal in mind. They violate and harm others just for the thrill of it. Like I mentioned, we all have that potential in us. The potential to harm others without explanation or reason. Dark psychology takes this potential to be difficult and complex to explain. Let us look at the 0.01% manipulators in dark psychology.

Predator - This is a person or persons who exploit, victimize, stalk, or coerce others using information in technology. They have desires and fantasies to control and get power. Predators can be of any age and gender who indulge in cyberstalker, cyberbully, internet troll, cyber-terrorist, online psychopath, or who engages in internet defamations.

Arsonist - This is a person who is obsessed with fire and its settings. These types of people have a history of physical and sexual abuse. Most arsonists are loners, have few peers, and are impressed by fire. They are ritualistic and set fires on a pattern. They get their targets and set it ablaze to get sexual arousal and feel proud.

Necrophilia - These are people with disorders and have a sexual attraction to dead people. They have a problem and get sexually attracted to things or corpses.

CHAPTER 3:

Historical Outline of Mental Manipulation

Every tree with sweet fruits hanging on its strong branches stemmed from a seed. Funny enough, even the trees with poisonous fruits came from tiny seedlings; they did not fall from the sky. Let us dig the ground together and understand where this villain called mental manipulation stemmed from. The birth of mental manipulation has to begin with the study by Jonathan Edwards, who discovered it in the 18th Century. It was during a crusade in Massachusetts when he discovered it accidentally. He found that by making Christians feel guilty and increasing the tension on them, they would always attend the meetings and submit completely.

Charles J. Finney also used this mental manipulation for four years in his ministry, and even today, many revivalists are using it on their Christians. As a result of the mental manipulation, one person attempted to take his life, and another committed suicide.

Most people confessed that they were also affected and always had suicidal feelings pushing them. Most preachers still manipulate their followers mentally intending to increase their followings especially the televised variety. Mental manipulation was first formulated on Christians, but scientists have also used it in the past.

Brain Phases

Pavlov, a Russian scientist, identified the states in which our brain responds to stimuli. The equivalent was the first phase, where our mind reacted the same to strong and weak stimuli. Paradoxical was the next phase where the mind favored weak stimuli than strong stimuli. Ultra-paradoxical is the last phase the brain adapts to conditioning. It turns positive behavior to negative and vice versa when conditioned. As you continue to manipulate the person mentally, the person becomes controlled. There are so many ways to manipulate a person mentally, but it mostly occurs in religion and politics. The first step is to work on a person's emotions until they are in complete anger, excitement, fear or tension. Mental manipulation intends to increase suggestibility and impair your judgment. When this manipulation is maintained, it compounds. Once the first stage is implemented, the manipulator has total control over the victim's brain, and he or she can replace the former mental programming with new patterns of his or her choice.

There are also more psychological weapons used to manipulate your mental capacities such as physical discomfort, fasting, mantra chanting as used in meditation, special lighting, intoxicating drugs, and sound effects, among many others. When these methods are used to manipulate you, they get the same outcome like in psychiatric treatment using the shock treatment or lowering a person's insulin with injection. Mental manipulation is different from hypnosis- mental manipulation is far stronger. However, you can mix the two and get powerful results. Even after many years have passed since it was discovered, our politicians, lawyers, and different people in society are using mental manipulation in our churches. Most of them do it with a goal in mind. They will communicate with a soft, patterned and well-paced voice to control your mind.

CHAPTER 4:

Techniques Used in Mental Manipulation

Persuasion Technique

Persuasion is controlling the human mind without the knowledge of the manipulated party. The manipulated party will change his or her opinion without being aware. This technique accesses your right mind, which is imaginative and creative, while the left side is rational and analytical. In persuasion, the perpetrator distracts your left brain and occupy it. It leaves you in an eyes-open altered state but still conscious, making you move from Beta awareness to Alpha. This technique is famous for politicians and lawyers.

Subliminal Programming

These are masked suggestions that can only be understood by your subconscious mind. They can be suggestions in audios, airbrushed visual suggestions, and flash images on your television quickly so that you do not consciously notice them. Some subliminal programming on audio makes suggestions on low volume. Your subconscious mind will notice these suggestions, but no one can monitor them even with equipment. The music we listen to can have a second voice behind it to program your mind. In 1984, a newsletter called Brain-Mind Bulletin that 99% of our activities are non-conscious.

Mass misuse - During mass meetings, the attendees go in and out of consciousness. If you have no idea, you cannot notice what is happening to you. It is a mental manipulation of the mass through vibrations. These vibrations produce Alpha, which makes the mass vulnerable. These make them accept any suggestion of the speaker as a command.

Vibrato - Vibrato is some effect installed on instrumental music or vocal, which makes people go in a distorted state of mind. In English history, some singers who had vibrato in their voices were not given chances to perform because of the effect they had on the public. Some listeners would have fantasies, mostly sexual fantasies.

Neurophone - Dr. Patrick Flanagan invented Neurophone. It is a device that can program your mind when it gets in contact with your skin. When this device gets in contact with your skin, you lose your sense and sight for a moment. It is because the skin has sensors for pain, touch, vibration, and heat. The message to manipulate your mind is played through Neurophone, which is connected and placed in the ceiling and no speakers. This message goes directly to the brain of the audience, and the manipulator can easily manipulate their mental state.

Medium for take-over - When you know how human beings function, you get the ability to control them. Medium take-over is happening in the televisions we watch. When people are put in a distorted state of mind, they function on the right brain, which releases brain opiates and makes you feel good, and you want it more.

The experience is the same as the one opium users feel. The broadcasts in our televisions induce the Alpha making us accept the broadcast easily. It makes viewers translate suggestions as commands. Every minute spent on watching television conditions us.

CHAPTER 5:

What Are the Signs of Manipulation As It Is Used In Today in the World (Practical Examples)

M anipulation happens in all kinds of relationships in our society. It happens between lovers, between pastors and their following, and politicians manipulate us as well, among many other relationships. In this chapter, we will look at the signs of manipulation in different relationships.

Churches

Manipulation in the church can occur in both ways. The people in the church leadership can manipulate their followers and vice versa. It is sad since most of us look at the church as the source of your peace. Most of us go for spiritual nourishment when we feel down from the church. How sad can it be if the church can be the source of your pain? Let us look at how the pastors can manipulate their followers.

1. Lack of open and honest conversations

In some churches, you are not allowed to ask questions. If you find yourself in such a situation, you are met with excuses or dismissal on not getting the information. It is okay when there are concerns not to divulge information that will interfere with the privacy of other members. The leaders should take responsibility for their actions and always be ready to explain to the members why there are certain rules. Church information should be open to its members, and there should be transparency.

2. Leaders never admit their mistakes

We can forgive our pastors for making mistakes. After all, they are human beings, but it is difficult to forgive them when they fail to communicate. Yes, I know what the Bible says about forgiveness, but remember, I am a human being too. When leaders refuse to admit to their mistakes and are always spinning their actions to fit those of a perfect lamb of God, they create a difficult situation. You should watch out for some recurring defensiveness in your church's leadership. You should also watch out if the church is masking some of its mistakes.

3. They use shame as an influence mechanism

Some churches in our community use shame to influence their members. They will shame their members for giving little money, shame them for missing the service and shame them for their actions. Even with no knowledge of the world, the Bible is clear that to those who belong to Christ, there is no condemnation.

Remember, none of those in the church leadership will sit on the judgment seat at the end of the world. Some of them act as if they have the final say on who will enter the gates of heaven. They will use the carrot and stick theory to manipulate you.

4. They are selective

First of all, you should understand that God created us all equally, and He accepts us the way we are. In some churches, they will restrict you to dress in a certain manner, they will choose people of a certain color, and they will force their members to follow some stipulated rules for them to fellowship in that church. The church should not have superficial lines but should be an all-inclusive place. The church should emulate Christ, who embraced all the rich such as Lazarus and the prostitutes, such as Mary Magdalene. Do not get me wrong; rules and regulations are important to run any organization but rules created to exclude a certain group of people in the wrong. Church leaders should know that they are servants.

Now I do not want you to think that pastors are evil for such actions above. You might find that some are not even aware of these manipulative actions, but others do it intentionally. Flipping the coin, pastors are also prone to manipulation. The church members can do it without the pastors realizing it. All the same, neither of the manipulations is acceptable. Let us look at the other side of the coin and find out how the church members can manipulate their pastors.

Compliments

Compliments are good as they encourage us and make us feel good. Now some members may use compliments to manipulate you. They will seek to influence your decisions in the church's agenda through flattery. You should watch out for such signs, as they are as bad as using criticism to bully another.

Criticisms

Well, you can never avoid criticism, especially if you have a leadership role. During conversations, some members will criticize your actions using their tone and sometimes body language. Always follow the church's rules and regulations and the teachings of the Bible. Be gentle when responding to such scenarios, and you will settle the manner amicably.

Silence

They tell us that silence is the best tool to silence manipulation, but it can also be a sign of manipulation. You find members giving you the silent treatment to control you. The pastor should be aware of this and should not carry the burden but instead should pray for the members.

Prayers

Pastors should take caution with the people they share with their burdens. They should protect themselves and their families from over-exposure. They should find trusted friends to share with their challenges, and even then, they should choose what is important to share and what is not.

Families

As we mentioned, earlier, manipulation happens in all kinds of relationships. It can be intentionally used or unintentionally, but in the end, the other party ends up doing something they did not want to do in the first place. In our homes, parents can manipulate their children, and the children can manipulate their parents as well. Children learn at an early age that they can get what they want through tantrums and when you give in, they get control. Away from the children. Now, what are the signs that teens are manipulating their caregivers?

1. Steamrolling

Teenagers make endless and repetitive requests that are meant to wear out the caregivers to get their way. They will use the 'can I' 'how about now' language all the time. The act like a broken record that keeps playing the same song repeatedly.

2. Lying

Teenagers love to tell little white lies or omitting some parts of the truth to get what they want. They leave out some details if given, would change your affirmation to their request. Most of them also collaborate on the small lies in case the parents communicate; they will have the same information and allow them their request.

3. Retaliation

Most teenagers do some hurtful things to retaliate for not getting their way. They will not clean their room; they will dress inappropriately, they will put on loud music; all these as an attempt to get even with you. It is difficult because you cannot yell at them to stop since they are no longer children, and most caregivers end up giving in to their demands to avoid these hurtful actions.

Caregivers can as well manipulate their children, and it is bad since the children are in their developing age, and it makes their life difficult. Briefly, let us look at the signs that a caregiver is manipulating the child.
- They do not give the child security and affirmation
- They are always critical.
- The caregiver always demands the attention of the child.
- The caregiver makes toxic jokes about the child.
- The caregiver does not allow the child to express their negative emotions
- The caregiver scares the child.

Politics

Politicians engage the emotional system of your brains to get political mileage. They use fear, disgust, and anger and never compassion or hope. Politicians never inspire us to work together for the common good of us all. They use anger, fear, and disgust to manipulate how we vote. They influence how we feel about other candidates and their policies. Most of us are never aware that we are being manipulated.

1. Informing you that the turn-out will be high

Politicians will tell you that they turn out will be high to motivate you to go to the polls. If they told you that the turn out would be low, most would not turn out since it depresses the efforts to go out and vote.

2. Public shaming

The politicians will never shame you publicly to safeguard their reputation and their votes, but they can use other means to make you feel bad for not voting. You would get ads and letters asking you what your relatives and friends would think of you if you did not vote. It will push you to vote.

3. Making promises or threats to follow up with you

It is natural for human beings to do things in the right way when their actions are under observation. In the 2010 US election, some people received a letter to encourage them to vote. Others received the same letter, but with an addition that they will be called to share their voting experience. It brought more voter turnout than the previous general election.

CHAPTER 6:

How to Recognize A Manipulator and What Are the Signs of Manipulation (Add A Lot of Details)

Each one of us has been manipulated in one way or the other. Some of us have been manipulated for many years without understanding that they are being manipulated. Recognizing a manipulator is hard since they manipulate you in secret. Manipulators are unscrupulous, skillful, and self-centered. They never leave behind fingerprints when they commit this crime, but the good thing is we can understand and predict this behavior if we know what we are looking for. How can you recognize a manipulator?

Manipulators undermine your conviction to grasp the reality

Manipulators are good at lying. They can insist that an episode happened, but it didn't, or they insist that it did happen, but in reality, it didn't happen. I know it sounds easy to escape such a trap, but they are so good at this tactic that they will make you question your sanity.

Their actions and words are dissimilar

Manipulators have a way with words. They will always tell you what will tick you, but their actions go in the opposite direction. They will promise to change, they will promise to support you, but when it comes to implementing their promises, they will act as if you are asking for a lot from them. They will insist on how blessed and lucky they are to have you in their life, but their actions will portray that you are a burden to them. You should be keen on this behavior because it also undermines your grasp of reality.

They are good at a guilt-tripping their victims

Have you ever met someone who made a mistake, but instead of owning up to their mistake, they made you feel guilty for their mistakes? Manipulators have mastered this art, and they will never allow you to complain of their wrong actions because when you do, they make you feel bad for bringing it up, and in cases where you keep it to yourself, they also make you feel bad for not bringing it up. In some cases, they will make you feel sorry for them by acting as the victim, yet they are on the wrong. They will use a tone of desperation or sometimes result in silent treatment to make you feel guilty for something bad they did.

They have an appetite for power

They have an arrogant attitude that makes them believe that they are superior to everyone else. They use this sense of superiority to control you and feel a sense of power. Their appetite for power is insatiable.

Does he or she raise his or her voice?

Manipulators have a misplaced sense of power and always feel entitled to everything. When things don't go as they had planned, they may result in raising their act, voice, or become aggressive. They do that to coerce you to agree with their plans or idea.

They use negative jokes to hurt you

Manipulators will make fun of your looks, your cooking, and your mode of communication in a masked manner to hide their real intentions. They do this to show superiority over you.

Sweet-talking

I know we all love to hear sweet words about ourselves and our deeds, but this is a different kind of sweet-talking. Manipulators' sweet talks have no truth in it. They use it to deceive you. We relate to people differently. For instance, the way you relate with your best friend is different from the way you relate with a stranger. Manipulators hasten connections by using sweet talks. At the same time, if you are observant, you will notice that their actions and sweet words do not match.

They take advantage of all weak spots

Manipulators are smart people and are aware of your weak spot through observation or talking you into divulging that information. They know all your insecurities and never hesitate to use them against you. They use that information to manipulate you instead of reassuring you and making you feel better.

They always have it worse than you do

We all have problems and difficult situations in this life. In a situation where you are sharing a problem with a manipulator, they never listen and make you feel better. They always have a worse problem than yours up their sleeve. They will make you feel bad for complaining because your problem does not legit to complain about.

They use charm and niceness

Manipulators may use charm to get sex or power. They do not struggle to use charm; it comes naturally to them.
Their conscious does not limit them to use it to hurt others. In most cases, they are good at studying your behavior, and with

time, they get to know your needs. They then give you what you needed to have you coiled in their little thumb.

They are fond of denying

Manipulators never admit their mistakes. If they wrong you and you bring it to their attention, they deny it. They never take responsibility for their mistakes or bad behaviors.

They use lies as a weapon

They have no problem with lying, as their conscience is impaired. They never miss a chance to get anything they need; instead, they use lies to get it. They lie by withholding information or distorting the truth.

Generosity with gifts

Some manipulators can be kind and generous. I know it sounds unbelievable, but you should already guess that they do so with an intent. They will shower you with gifts and give you favors to get bigger favors from you shortly. You might think that these acts are their way of expressing love, but if you pay attention to their character, you will find out otherwise.

They use compliments in excess

Manipulators will shower you with compliments in excess. They will flatter you at every opportunity. Compliments are good, and they make us feel good about ourselves, but when you notice they are too much, it is important to ask yourself what that person wants from you.

Forced teaming

Manipulators will act like you are in the same team to create a notion of unity and togetherness with their victims. They will often use the word we, but instead of you feeling comfortable with it, you will feel discomfort, and you will not have the will to refuse because you will appear rude.

Signs of Manipulation

We already know how you can recognize a manipulator, but how can you tell if you are being manipulated? Let us find out the signs of manipulation.

Home court advantage

As we already know, manipulation is all about control. Manipulators take you away from familiar grounds to unfamiliar ones to have an advantage over gaining control over you. A manipulator will take you on a date at his favorite restaurant, make you hang out with his friends. They do that to feel in control because it is easy to control a person who is not comfortable with the surroundings.

Plain old bullying

A manipulator will bully you with his or her actions to do something. They will make a request, but their tone of voice and body language indicates a threat in case you fail to do it. Once you do what they had requested, they will tell you that you did not have to do it and make you look like you had a choice, and you did not.

Tugging on your heartstrings

A manipulator will make you feel bad for saying no. In normal situations, people come to common ground when making a decision, and it is acceptable if you are not comfortable with some ideas, but in manipulation, you have no right to say no because when you do, the manipulator will make you feel like you are the worst person on earth.

Emotional blackmail

In manipulation, the manipulators will make you do stuff for them with a condition. For instance, your boyfriend might ask you to visit his aging grandma, and when you refuse because of different reasons, they can threaten to harm themselves.

Playing the victim

In manipulation, the perpetrator does something wrong but acts like the victim. They will make you apologize for their mistakes. The manipulator is always helpless and hurt, and this makes you feel like you are the bad one in the relationship. They make their victims feel bad, and at the same time, they avoid being accountable for their mistakes.

Gaslighting

Gaslighting is a manipulation tactic that makes you feel like you are going mad.
 The manipulator will say ugly things to you and then pretend that they didn't; they will twist information, pretend like they did not say some of it, leave out some vital information and make you think you are going dander. When they apply this

technique for a long time, you feel as if you cannot trust yourself and your thinking. You stop relying on your judgment to make decisions and start relying on theirs.

CHAPTER 7:

How to Defend Yourself from Those Who Want To Manipulate Us

Manipulative people tend to disguise their interests as one`s interests. In other words, they are the kind of people who will believe that their opinions, as well as facts, are the best and yours doesn't count. They will attract any form of attention and take credit in places where they don't deserve it. They are the kind of people who will tell everyone how incompetent you are. They will then work on improving your skills so as they can use you to get more credit. If you fail to change the way they want, they will ruin your life. It is worth noting that they are the kind of people who will help you so as they can control you as well. In other words, they will force you to change not to better your life but so as they can use you. They will do all they can to ensure that they will keep you from outgoing them. They can`t allow you to outshine them although they will pretend to be helping you. It is worth noting that once you enable manipulative people in your life, they are tough to get rid of. In other words, they will flip flop issues and make your success path to be slippery and confusing. They are the kind of people who will ensure that they have used all your efforts for their benefits. Thus, it is wise to avoid them and get rid of their schemes and plans. Take a look at some of the techniques you can use to prevent their projects.

Ignore everything they do and Say

When you are dealing with manipulative people, one of the biggest mistakes you can do is correct them. In other words, a manipulative person thinks that his way of doing things in the best, and there is no way it can be changed. They have their tactics that they believe they are the best and all the other people under their custody can`t have better ideas than they do. In other words, the art of correcting them should be the aspect you need to avoid. However, what you need to do is to ignore everything they do or say. Also, you should work hard and ensure that they don`t realize or understand the things that trigger you most. The aspect is linked to the fact that once they have known the things that trigger you, they will use them to influence all your actions. Uniquely if they can identify the things you love most, they will use them as a bait to manipulate or somewhat control all your activities. One of the best strategies to avoid the manipulative aspect is to ignore their ideas. What you need to do is to delete all their ideas in your minds. Don't show concerned with what they want you to do? The aspect is linked to the fact that they will ensure that they have corned you and ensure that they have the credit they want from you. If they happen to be your relatives or your bosses, you may agree with what they say but turn around and do your things. At first, they will be pissed off by your actions and end up ignoring you once they realize that you aren't interested in what they believe. However, if you will accidentally do what they like doing, they will end up manipulating you.

Hit their Center of Gravity

It is worth noting that manipulative people will always use their strategies to ensure that they are against you. For instance, they may hold past actions over your head and tell your friends to turn against you. They are the kind of people who will become your friends to your loved ones so as they can sue them to ill-treat you. They may even get a step further to reward your friends and ensure that they all turn against you. At such moments, they will then pretend to be good friends so as you can tell them all your secrets. They will, in turn, utilize such secrets to ensure that they have controlled all your actions. The aspect is linked to the fact that if they identify your past mistakes as well as the things you won`t like to know by others, you will probably do whatever they ask so as they can instill the secret. The best thing for you to do is to turn the tables and ensure that the deals you have with them turn out to be miserable. If you have an experience with them, you can ignore all their attempts of be-friending you and close all the lope holes where they can understand about your secrets. The aspect is linked to the fact that they will lack a chance of manipulating you. You need to find their center of gravity. In other words, you need to identify the things that cause havoc in them. Pinpoint their strengths and work on reducing them to ashes. In other words, if they use words to convince people, ensure that you didn't offer any listening ear to them. Some use parties to influence their victims. Thus, you need to avoid such parties or any offers they give to people so as they can win. Some may have a deeper understanding of a particular aspect of life. Maybe it is a specific resource they control. What you need to do is to avoid all their strategies and ensure that you didn't close their paths. The aspect is critical in the sense that you will be in a good position of avoiding the things that could escalate their manipulative elements in your life.

Trust the Judgments you make

What you need to understand is that you are the best and whatever decision you are about to make is yours, and no one can do the best as you do. The aspect is critical in the sense that you will be in a good position avoiding the art of being manipulated. In other words, you will avoid cases where someone is using your capabilities to explore your emotions as well as the things you like. You need to define your life and trust your decisions. You don't have to get approval from people so as you can move on with what you think will work out the best for you. You need to understand that your boundaries are your beliefs. In other words, you need to set your limits and stick to them. The aspect is critical in the sense that it helps an individual to prevent all the manipulative people from affecting their lives. In other words, if you are able to set healthy boundaries, the people who are around, you won`t have a chance to manipulate you. The art is linked to the fact that you won`t open up and allow manipulative people have credit over your efforts.

Try to Fit in

As you cope up or live with manipulative people, you need to keep re-inventing yourself and try as much as possible to fit in. One of the significant characteristics of manipulative people is that they like a situation where you are using all your efforts to please them. For instance, they will love a job where you come and clean their houses and make them happy. They will want a position where you wake up in the morning and prepare their offices for them. They will also prefer a situation where you leave your duties and ensure that they are first fixed. You don't have to meet all their, please. However, you can try and fit in their desires but don't allow them to carry you. The aspect is linked to the fact that their ideas are aimed at manipulating you. Also, if you avoid doing what they want, your life might be miserable. The aspect is linked to the fact that most of these manipulative people are your bosses. In other words, they are the kind of people you need to work under so as you can excel. Thus, try and fit in their rules but don't give in to their demands. In other words, you can look for different ways of fixing their applications rather than using the techniques as well as the strategies they have identified. The aspect is critical in the sense that your actions will act as eye-openers in the desire to change. If you can achieve their demands using other means they may end fearing you. The aspect is linked to the fact that they will understand that they aren't the only people who can come up with such ideas. Thus, they will be cautious in terms of their actions and demands. However, you don't have to show them how sharp you are. They may end up ill-treating you. However, if you are wise in the way you conduct things, they may fear you and avoid cases where they will ill-treat you. The aspect is linked to the fact that there will be a sense of self-respect that will emerge in between you.

CHAPTER 8:

Hypnosis and Self-Hypnosis

Hypnosis refers to an induction of a state of consciousness where a person loses their power of voluntary actions and is highly responsive to any direction as well as suggestion. It is one of the useful therapy that allows one to suppress their memories and will enable the modification of their behaviors. Self-hypnosis, on the other hand, refers to an instinctively happening state of mind that can be illustrated as an elevated state of fixated concentration. In other words, it changes the way a person thinks, kick out bad habits as well as control themselves. It is one of the means of introducing the art of relaxations and distressing the day to day life. The two aspects are critical in the sense that they allow one mind to re-write or rather reprogram the subconscious. The element is crucial in the sense that it will enable one to relax and bypass the issues that are affecting someone hence introducing some positive mindsets.

In most cases, the ideas as well as aspects instilled in one`s minds are positive and encourages one to re-think more and act differently. It is one of the best ways of enhancing the efficacy of self-suggestion and plays the due role of being the suggester and the suggested. In other words, the aspect allows one mind to indicate to itself the things that ought to be carried out or be done for a solution to be viable. Thus, the two aspects are very crucial in life.

Take a look at some of the importance of both Hypnosis and Self-hypnosis.

Improving Deep Sleep

Several studies have been used to explore the effect of hypnosis on one`s sleep. In most of these studies, the participants were asked to report back on how well or poorly they slept after hypnosis. In most cases, victims who have sleep issues have reported improving after anesthesia. One of the effects of hypnosis is that it allows the minds of an individual to relax and empties all the negative thinking. The aspect is critical in the sense that it will enable one to develop some understanding of cooling as well as relaxation. Thus one is able to sleep well and wakes up while more active. It is worth noting that sleeping is a state of mind. Also, the art of sleeping is directly proportional to the level of one`s tiredness. In other words, if one is tired, there are chances that they will be able to sleep well. However, with age, the aspect of sleeping tends to reduce. The inactivity that tends to increase with age tends to decrease the art of sleeping. In other words, the elders in society have sleep issues. The technique can be linked to the fact that most of them are inactive during the day, and they may remain active for the entire day. Thus, their rate of sleeping may tend to lower. However, with hypnosis, such cases are rare. The art is linked to the fact that hypnosis allows the mind of an individual to be emptied and re-written in a new way. The technique creates some sense of relaxation that will enable one to sleep well. One of the merits of hypnosis is that it doesn't have any side effects. It is worth noting that numerous drugs are used to induce sleep in an individual.

In most cases, some of these drugs are addictive, such that people who are used to them can`t get sleep without taking such drugs. The other aspect is that apart from addiction, the drugs may increase the hangover issues that affect people who are addicted to drug abuse. Thus it one of the safest means of solving problems of sleep.

It eases symptoms of Irritable Bowel Syndrome.

Various studies have been carried out to identify the effects of hypnosis in one`s life. There have been reports that clients with Irritable bowel syndrome have greatly improved after a consecutive 12 weeks of hypnosis. It is worth noting that the improvement occurred even after months of inductive therapy. Hypnosis, as well as self-hypnosis, are critical in the sense that they reduce the cost of healthcare to the entire society. The other merit is that it is one of the therapies that doesn't attract any attention in terms of causing chaos. However, hypnosis creates an environment that creates an excellent mental picture that tends to capture the attention of one`s mind hence bringing a healing effect. The art of emptying one`s mind and allowing the state of relaxation will enable one to attract more positivity. The art of being positive creates some sense of enjoyment in one`s mind hence bringing about a healing effect.

Calming Nerves

The nerves of an individual are always active. However, there are situations where the minds of an individual need to relax and lower anxiety. In most cases, when one is afraid, their hair stands, some may sweat or even shaking. At such moments, the nerves are active, and there are cases where operations are required for such nerves to be examined. However, hypnosis helps the mind as well as the nerves to relax and brings down the art of being anxious. The other aspect that affects the brain of an individual is expectations.

In most cases, the expectations that people have tend to cause some sense of alarm in an individual. The aspect may be so intense that the individual may develop what is called anxiety-related disorder. The victim is always anxious about what will happen in the future. The art causes the minds to over-think and in the long –run increases the trait if being over-expectant. However, hypnosis is one of the therapies that are effective in lowering anxiety.

Treatment of life-style Diseases such as Hypertension

Most of the life-style diseases that affect people tend to originate from the state of mind. For instance, anxiety increases the rate at which the heart pumps blood. In most cases, when the price of pumping blood increases, the pressure of blood increases within the narrow vessels. The aspect can be dangerous as if the pressure reaches the capillaries in the head. Blood pressure is thus a state of mind that needs to be challenged. In other words, the incidence of mental illness is directly proportional to the increase in blood pressure. Therefore, the treatment of blood of these conditions requires more attention to the minds. The aspect means that if the accounts of such an individual are allowed to relax, the chances are that cases of blood pressure lower, and there is a healing effect that is noted.

Memory Improvement

As outlined earlier, one of the aspects of hypnosis is that it allows the minds of an individual to refresh or rather to be re-programmed. The re-creation is essential in improving one`s memory. It is worth noting that once the accounts are upgraded, there is a healing effect that is instilled. In most cases, the negative aspect of the brain tends to lower. It is worth noting that a positive mind brings some sense of relaxation in the accounts. One thinks well hence the ability to remember many aspects. For instance, in a class, the difference between a bright student and a dull one is the attitude over a particular subject. For example, students who fear mathematics tend to develop some sense of negativity towards teaching.

In most cases, the victim can't pass on such a subject. The aspect is linked to the fact that the victim has developed a negative mindset that robs one's ability to remember. On the other hand, positive students tend to have an increased ability to recognize aspects of the same subject. The element causes one to have a better memory. Thus, the art of developing a positive mindset after a session of hypnosis plays a critical role in boosting the mind of an individual.

Improves Concentration and Focus

A relaxed mind is more attentive than a tired one. One of the most important aspects of hypnosis is that it allows the mind to relax and reprogram itself. In most cases, as the brain reprogram itself, some points are eliminated. Most of the elements that are removed are more contradictory ideas as well as issues that hinder a person's prosperity. After a session of relaxation, or rather hypnosis, the minds are rejuvenated and less depressed. The feeling of anxiety lowers, and one gets ready for grasping more ideas. In other words, the art of concentration and focus improves after a session of hypnosis. The art of phobia and other mental related disorders are eliminated. Also, the art of healing gastrointestinal disorders as well as high blood pressure causes the minds to relax and focus on other vital issues. It is one of the best therapy of topics such as low self-esteem as well as stress disorders. Thus, the minds are allowed to relax and heal. The rejuvenations give the mind time to heal and prepare for learning. Therefore, if you are willing to improve on your studies, you need to have some sessions of hypnosis and improve on your focus, let alone concentration.

CHAPTER 9:

Emotional Manipulation (How Its Mechanism Works)

S ome people are always lucky in that they can get what they want at any time the need arises. Sometimes they do so at the expense of others, this, however, is achieved via access to the emotional bank. They can influence your thoughts or emotions to their advantage and leave you a victim and vulnerable. Emotional manipulation, therefore, involves access to someone and influencing them for information or any other favors through their emotions. It sucks and it is unethical once you realize what has been done to you. Do not get confused, there are two sides to emotional manipulation. There is an ethical and unethical side. What feels like betrayal is the unethical one. However, mastering emotional intelligence plays a barrier role to these manipulations and keeps you in a safe spot. In this chapter, the focus is on how emotional manipulation is attained and the mechanisms behind it.

Owning space

The main aim of emotional manipulation is to make you lose control of your emotions. It will involve making you stagger with emotions which on the other hand will make you even more vulnerable. Advantage will be taken and they will access you and get all they wanted from you. If there existed a lock to the emotions, I am sure everybody would have their emotions locked away and unlocked only to intimate relationships or where your emotions will be valued. To make sure you are off the steering with your emotions, manipulators will invite you to a place where they know it is new to you but familiar to them. This will keep you off balance, the new environment will give him or her the dominance and feeling of being in control. You are new to the place and the manipulator will take advantage of the window between adaptability and regaining control.

Your words against you

How you talk or react speaks volumes and emotions can be passed along. Manipulators like a talkative person since it is easier to access them due to the link provided; speaking out. If you are the introvert type or a conservative person it takes more effort to make you open up. Introverts would require tailored questions that will be well planned and will give you away from one by one. The manipulator makes sure the questions are aimed at the emotional state. Personal questions will open you up and you will start speaking with feelings, this is an indicator that manipulation is taking place and it is working. By asking simple and tailored questions that mostly are personal or involve something we like hobbies, interests among others will lead to saturation with emotions.

A master manipulator will take advantage of the situation and make us of the questions to establish your beliefs, strengths, and weaknesses without you realizing it.

Guilt

Kind-hearted victims are easily vulnerable to emotional manipulation. Guilt will be used against you, especially if you are so sensitive you may end up giving in to their demands. Guilt will either make you give in or feel bad about yourself. For instance, you may both agree on something and when the time comes to complete the deal the manipulators will pretend to forget or even act as victims of your actions. By doing so they will be finding your soft spot and once they find it will be the target of manipulation. Guilt and sympathy will be served to you, if you are not strong enough you will fall for the play. They will influence you through that guilt since you will be under their spell and since you now believe they are the victims you will do all they ask just to make sure your 'victims' do not suffer anymore.

Positive and negative emotions

Emotions of sadness or happiness can also be a pathway for emotional manipulation. An emotional manipulator will play with your psychology, he or she will show you that what you might be going through is nothing compared to what they have going on in their lives. By doing this, they try to exalt you and win your trust. If you fall for that and believe there are more needy people than you in the world then you will loosen up and think that you are selfish. You will no longer focus on your big problem, rather you will focus on their 'big unfortunate events' since you will now feel pitiful. Once you trust them, then you give them a key to your emotional bank and surely they will use it against you. Once you trust them, you might end up offering yourself to assist them, that, however, was their plan from the start; they will have attained their goal.

Anger

Anger is another emotion that can be used to induce emotional manipulation. Some people are natural peacemakers, they avoid confrontations and conflicts in all ways possible. Once a manipulator realizes you are this type of person, he or she will use anger, aggressive language or raise his or her voice or even drop several threats. These aggressive techniques are tailored just to make tick. The secret behind this aggressive approach is to induce fear and discomfort so that you can give in hastily without taking a second to think through. Once you give in to their demands they now get control over you and now can manipulate you in whatever direction or way that pleases them. They use this opportunity to get what they wanted from you since you will be cooperative earing to bring another instance of acute aggression.

Self-discipline and confidence

Being self-driven and confident is a very strong barrier to the effects of emotional manipulation. With the right mindset, you become less vulnerable to emotional manipulation attacks. Insecure and sensitive people are the easiest target for emotional manipulators. They are easily spotted and accessible, they put their needs behind those of others and are often feeling the need to please. All a manipulator needs is to be caring, sensitive and with an urge to help out. The needy part of sensitive people exposes them and the emotional manipulator will see it as a gate pass to influencing your thoughts, perceptions, and feelings to his or her advantage. With time the emotions break open and they are exploited easily since the manipulator was disguised as a caring and sensitive person. As the saying goes, birds of a feather flock together; the feeling of sharing the same trait will open them up for manipulation without their knowledge.

Surprises

Negative surprises is also another mechanism used to keep people off balance. When bombarded with the new unexpected news that comes with a limited timeframe will lead to panic. As you panic, you get little time or none to think of a counter move. They may be good enough to trap you with suggestions as they pretend to help yet it is a plan made to make you unstable both psychologically and emotionally. Once you become unstable and overwhelmed by the sudden change of events it becomes their opportunity to influence your decisions and any other emotion they are interested in. They may even consider making more moves that will bind your relationship with him, her or them so that they can utilize that window of opportunity created by the panic moment. You may not realize it since they appear to be assisting whereas they are using you for their benefits.

Criticism

Criticism is also a tool for emotional manipulation. The manipulator will say bad things of you, ridicule you or even dismiss you. He or she will make sure her mission of dismantling you succeeds. Once you have had enough you end up off balance and believe they are much superior compared to the inferior you. You will feel so down and their opinions will stick. Once you are in this state you are vulnerable. The manipulator will make sure you understand that you can never be good at anything no matter what you do or invest in. This will get into you and you will be emotionally distressed. You will feel hurt and not worthy of anyone's help. They will then pretend to have answers to your problems. He or she will give you tips and suggestions that are so genuine looking and constructive. Once these well-outlined answers transform you and get you out of it they threw you will worship them. Once they have your attention they can then make you do what they want or influence you.

Doubt

Doubt and uncertainty are also other forms of leverage in emotional manipulation. You will receive a silent treatment until you start doubting your actions or words that you may have used the last time. The manipulators will do this deliberately to stir up the feeling of doubt, once you give in and break the silence by acting as the cause of the silence treatment will be a good chance to be taken advantage of. This creates a window of opportunity and they will manipulate you.

Ignorance

Pretending to be ignorant of your duties will also get things done. You may want to do something but you want it done by someone else, let us say your spouse. She or he will note something is off and will try to make it right but you pretend to be good with it but since they know it has to be right they will do it anyway.

CHAPTER 10:

How to Learn To Use Manipulation to Your Advantage

Manipulation is something that we cannot master overnight. The closer you get to a person the easier the process of manipulation becomes. Making people fall into your traps and flow with your ideas making it seem it was theirs in the first place is a manipulative move. Getting things done efficiently would be our greatest achievement but when we get assistance and it is done perfectly, we feel more graceful and happy. With the power of manipulation which would take some time to master, you can swing things around to fit your needs and desires. In this chapter, the focus is on the ways that can be apprehended and used to make sure you gain the skills of manipulation and use them accordingly; to suit your needs. Manipulation strategies will require some cold-heartedness since may involve hurting other peoples' emotions without caring. The focus is on what you can get and the method does not necessarily care about what your emotions are or what might be at stake.

Emotional intelligence

Learn emotional intelligence and practice it. To access people's actions and feelings, emotions make it easier. Emotions are able to access the mind; subconsciously and we react subconsciously. Unless you have mastered the art of emotional intelligence and self-discipline you cannot avoid an attack on the emotions' bank; the subconscious mind. The subconscious mind will act fast and without the awareness and consent of the conscious mind. This, however, makes the bridge to manipulation; the manipulator will now be in a position to access your feelings and play around with them so that you can tune to the song being played. Make sure you harness the power of emotional intelligence and be in a position to radiate the products of the same. Once you master that, manipulation will become a piece of cake and you will influence people's thoughts, feelings, and emotions to your liking.

Charms and flirts

Master the art of charms and flirts. People that like you without effort are likely to do anything to get noticed by you; the charming guy. Use charms to gain popularity and love from people, let people talk about how good you are and likable. To this, trait and image made out there add a touch of fluttery to spice things up; you will prepare lands that you can garden any time as long as you use the right approach to smoothen things. Manipulating people that have a crush on you becomes easy and when you keep your sexuality off the table and flirt, you will access control of people who are vulnerable. People with self-esteem are mostly people-pleasing and therefore when you show interest they will easily fall into your arms. Use this opportunity to make them work towards your goal or assist you in any way that pleases you.

Invest in self-confidence

Learn the power of being confident in yourself. People are likely to believe you more when you are confident in yourself and what you say. To win people overuse the right posture and words accompanied by a handful of confidence and magic will happen. What you say to them will not matter, your actions rather will be the target to scrutiny and once you win them over you will have their loyalty to yourself. Once they believe that what you do is for their benefit and you let it stick to them with a lot of confidence, they will participate even though it is against their desires.

Act

Be an actor, pretend to be something you are not so as to fit in. Learn how to use trust to open up people. Act needy and tell someone a very private and personal experience, they will be triggered to share theirs. It takes a lot of courage and trust to let go off of some of such private issues. Once you win the trust of the individual you are a step ahead in manipulation. The victim might not know the validity of the story if you act right and blend in feelings with the story and experience. The victim also might not be aware of the manipulation since the exchange of the experiences.

Empathy

Empathy will make people trust you since you seem to understand what they feel. Understanding people and giving them a shoulder to cry on is emotional support. People will trust you with their problems and insecurities as long as you maintain the relationship. Be a good listener and show care and understanding. The feeling of having someone by your side in times of crisis will make you do all to maintain him or her. Use the opportunity to make sure they tune to your beat. They might not realize they are helping out rather them it will be an act of kindness.

Apprenticeship

Working closely with a master manipulator will also get you a ton of skills in manipulation. You will learn by observing and apprenticeship. Theoretical knowledge learned sometimes proves hard to apply to the field. Therefore, learning the way to manipulate people under an expert as you watch it being done, chances are that you will become very good at it. You learn even more modified techniques that will not be covered in the theoretical class. Practice makes perfect therefore learning under an expert and practicing what he or she does will get you started. If you are this lucky to have a manipulator around make use of him or her to achieve the skills of manipulation.

Mirroring

Mirroring actions or postures of the target individuals may bring synchronization between you two. Manipulators try to imitate your actions and posture both voluntary and involuntary ones. This will help open up the target individual and also show them that you are aware of their insecurities if any exists. Not only does mirroring involve the postures but also the words said. Repeating what has been said lastly with an agreeing tone will show that you were attentive and interested in the topic. Showing interest in what they have to say will make sure they do the same when your turn comes.

CHAPTER 11:

What Communication And Verbal Skills Need To Be Developed To Improve Persuasion And Manipulation Skills?

T here is nothing as important as being able to communicate effectively. One has to be able to verbally communicate in a way that people around them understand. People will believe and put their trust in someone who has effective communication skills. This is because they know how to speak to everyone depending on their levels of understanding. There are those types of competencies that one must have in order for them to be able to communicate effectively. A manipulator needs to have verbal skills in order for them to be able to communicate effectively with their victims. Being able to speak is more than just speaking. You are required to ensure that you convey the information you need to communicate to someone and they understand it. When they understand and respond the way you would want them to, that is when you will be able to say that you have communicated. It is important for a manipulator to understand that in order for them to use the communication skills to manipulate their victims without experiencing any communication problem.

Fortunately, all these skills can be learned or nurtured. Manipulators need to, therefore, ensure that they have the required skills for them to use when manipulating people. I have discussed some of the skills below.

Listening Skills

A manipulator needs to be a good listener if they want to be able to communicate with other people. They need to pay very close attention to the people they want to manipulate in order for them to be able to learn about their weaknesses and be able to use them against them. Active listening is very important since you will be able to capture all the required information for your own benefit. It is important for a manipulator to be able to learn the language that the victims understand. This will be of great help in ensuring that they do not use a complex language, which they will not understand.

An active listener will be able to listen to the recipient without judging them. When the manipulator judges the recipient, they will not be able to trust them. This will make them keep the information you need for themselves. To win their trust, you need to make sure that you pay attention to them as they speak. By doing all this, they will be able to give the information you require not knowing that you will use the same information to manipulate them.

Open Communication

Open communication is all about first impressions. The way one communicates with you the first time you meet helps you to judge their ability to communicate or not. How a manipulator communicates the first time they meet people will, therefore, determine whether they will be able to manipulate the recipient or not. A manipulator, therefore, needs to ensure that they have the required ability to communicate with the recipients. This will be of great help when they want to win them over to their side. Being open with communication will help you to be able to ensure that the victims gain their trust in you which will make them also open up to you. Your goal as a manipulator is to ensure that they give you as much information as they can which you will later use against them. This will make it easy for you to be able to persuade them or manipulate them.

Reinforcement

The use of reinforcement is a very common technique when one wants to use communication effectively. Manipulators can use it to improve their communication with the victim. They will be required to use encouraging words as well as gestures that are non-verbal when communicating with the victims in order for you to be able to make friends with them. This helps you as a manipulator to build a great rapport with them, which enables you to win their trust.

You will engage them in discussions and encourage them to keep opening up to you. Whenever they are down, you will need to be there to reassure them that all will be well. This will help you a lot when manipulating them since they will feel obligated to help you since you were also there for them when they needed you. You will, therefore, be able to easily manipulate them without experiencing any challenges.

Questioning

It is through questions that we are able to get information about various things. You will be able to get clarity for various issues when you question. A manipulator needs this skill too. They will use it to question their victims and get all the information they may need from them. This will give you a chance to be able to know their strengths and weaknesses which will in return help you to manipulate them. As a manipulator, you can choose to use either open or closed questions. A closed question is those that will give you either a yes or a no. an open one is one that the victim will need to explain their answers or discuss them. The best type of question to use in this case is the open one. This is because it will give you room to give you as much information as possible. A manipulator should, therefore, utilize these questions to ensure that they use the best opportunity to manipulate their victims.

Reflecting and Clarity

Reflection is normally used when one needs clarity on the things another person said. They translate the information given by another person into a simpler language that they can understand. A manipulator can use this opportunity to distort the information they give to the manipulator. They will ensure that the victim understands what manipulators can use to manipulate them. The information they give their victims is contrary to what the speaker said. This will help them to be able to easily manipulate the victim into following what they want.

Negotiation Skills

Negotiation skills refer to helping people to reconcile with or agree with each other's ideas. Negotiation is meant to make sure that people are living in peace and harmony especially at the workplace. A manipulator can use negotiation skills to make their victims agree with him. He will share ideas and ensure that the people they want to manipulate agree to them. This will work very well since most of the ideas they will be sharing will be manipulative. They will be for their own selfish gain. By the time, the victims realize it; they will have already been manipulated and will not be able to come out of it easily.

Importance of Developing Communication and Verbal Skills in Manipulation

Communication and verbal skills are important for any manipulator. This is because of how one communicates dictates whether they will be able to manipulate their victims or not.

Through communication, a manipulator will be able to derive information from their victims which they to manipulate them later.

Through communication, a manipulator is able to learn the strengths and weaknesses of their victims, which they use to manipulate them. They will use their weaknesses to make them follow all the instructions that they give. Manipulators do not people who are aware of themselves because it is not easy to manipulate them.

The manipulators also use communication to earn the trust of their victims. They have to use a good language, which they understand in order for their victims to trust them. These manipulators will be there to comfort their victims when they need them with encouraging words. By doing this, they are able to win their trust and manipulate them the sympathy in the future. The manipulators need to, therefore, use the best language for them to win people to their side.

Another importance of communication is that manipulators are good negotiators. They will use the appropriate language to make their victims fall prey to their trick to manipulate them. They will make sure that every information they get from the victim against them.

A manipulator will also be able to give clear instruction, which will be understood by their victims. For a manipulator to be able to manipulate them, they have to ensure that they understand the instructions and follow them as expected.

They will also be able to use communication and verbal skills to influence the victims of manipulation to their side. The ability to influence them is what will help them to win their trust, which in return enables them to be able to manipulate them.

A manipulator should, therefore, ensure that they learn the communication and verbal skills in order for them to be able to manipulate their victims effectively. This is because their art of manipulation is the one that will determine whether they will be able to manipulate them or not. Without communication, a manipulator would not be able to persuade, negotiate and even question the victims into manipulating them. It is therefore important for manipulators to sharpen their verbal communication in order for them to be able to succeed in manipulation.

CHAPTER 12:

How to Use Manipulation to Manipulate, Persuade and Influence People

We all find manipulating other people's minds unethical. This is because we consider it as playing with people's feelings as well as thoughts and emotions in order for it to benefit us alone. That is considered a very selfish move. Manipulators know how to play their cards well. They will make sure that they use all the available techniques to manipulate the targeted people. Whether manipulation is unethical or not mostly depends on an individual. This is because we are the ones with the final decision as to whether we should allow them to manipulate us or not.

One is therefore required to evaluate themselves every often in order for them to ensure that they have the required skills for them to be able to avoid manipulators. In this chapter, I am going to discuss some of the many manipulation techniques that one can use to manipulate, persuade and influence people.

Fear and Relief Technique

Fear and relief is a technique that is said to be very efficient when it comes to playing with other people's emotions. A manipulator is only required to instill some fear on an individual, which immediately makes them vulnerable. At the time when they are vulnerable, the manipulator does anything they want in their favor. The manipulator manipulates the individual at this point since they know that the victim will do anything to get out of the fearful situation.

The only challenge that the manipulator might encounter when using this technique is identifying the things that make them fear. They will, therefore, need to keep fearful situations to the every now and then until when they will identify it. The manipulators succeed in this situation since most people hate situations that make them fear. They would anything to make sure that they get out of the situation.

An example of how this technique is used is when the media wants to keep its viewers following the channel. They will put up a juicy headline, which will keep the viewers glued on the screen waiting for it. The reporter will then keep reporting that they need to keep watching the program in order for them to get the juicy news. Everyone will keep watching in the hope that the program will still come. With fear and relief techniques, the manipulator is expected to instill fear until when they see that the manipulator is about to give up. It is at this point that they will be able to relieve them of the pressure that they are going through which makes them less stressful. The fearful situation that they have been through makes them obey the manipulator's orders anytime they give them since they would not want to go back to the situation they were in before.

Guilty Approach Technique

Through the guilty approach technique, the manipulator makes their prey guilty in order for them to be able to manipulate them. They will make sure that they blame them for things they did not do. One will want to compensate the manipulator without the knowledge that they will are about to be manipulated. A manipulator has to however make sure that their target is someone who is prone to feeling guilty.

Once you make the person guilty, you will be able to swing them in any direction since they are willing to do anything to make sure that you forget the things that they did to you. It works so perfectly since according to the victim, they will compensate for the moments that they were not nice to you but for the manipulator, it will be time to use them for their selfish gain. The guilt approach technique, therefore, works so well when one wants to influence other people since the victim will be feeling an obligation to make it up to you for the trouble they caused you. Little do they know that the manipulator was waiting for such a moment to strike?

Playing the Victim

This type of technique is somehow similar to the guilty approach technique. Playing the victim may however work against you if not careful when implementing it. You would be required to ensure that you do not overuse it. The trick is normally to ensure that you make the targeted person feel bad about a given situation. You will be required to ensure that the person actually made the mistake but for you, playing the victim shall be an exaggeration. The victim will feel bad about it and will want to compensate it by doing something different for you. They will, therefore, be nice to you, which will help the manipulator to use them to achieve her goals.

Love Bombing Technique

We all like it when we feel loved by the people around us. We will all appreciate it when the people around us make us feel appreciated and loved. That is why manipulators use love and attention to manipulate people.

This technique is mostly used for the purposes of manipulating people emotionally. A manipulator will mostly give a lot of attention to their targeted individual. They will show them a lot of affection, which would make them, not suspect anything from the manipulator. By doing this, they will be setting up a trap for them. They will be laying the ground, which they will use for their manipulation purposes. When the right time comes, they are able to easily execute their plan. This means that by the time they realize that you are manipulating them; they will have already been influenced to a place of no return.

Bribery Technique

This technique is said to work like a charm. This is because you will reward someone out of nowhere and they will automatically want to return the favor in a different way. It is an easy job since you are only required to find out what your victim needs and you get them exactly that. You will only be expected to look as genuine as possible. This will make the person really happy such that if you ever mention that you need anything, they will not hesitate to get it for you. By doing this, you will be able to make demands from them as many times as possible without them noticing that you are manipulating them. Through this technique, you will have influenced people to your system, which they may find it difficult to exit.

Becoming a Good Listener

A manipulator knows that people need good listeners in their lives. A good listener earns people's trust so easily. This is because they will come out as being very caring and concerned. This makes the victim trust them completely. A manipulator cannot manipulate people before gaining their trust. Once you have their trust, it will be very easy to manipulate them. You will only be required to discuss with them a few things that you may be going through and without even questioning, they will reciprocate for it since you were there for them before. Through the trust, the manipulator will be able to manipulate them for a long time without the victim noticing.

In as much as a manipulator uses these skills to manipulate, persuade and influence people, they all need to be good in some skills.

Some of the skills have been discussed below.

- They need to have excellent verbal communication skills. No one will listen to someone who cannot communicate clearly. You would need to be able to express yourself well if at all you want people to listen to you. Most manipulators have mastered this skill very well which helps them to prey on people without them noticing. When one is good in communication, they are able to easily prey on the victims with the language that they understand. The victims will, therefore, understand the manipulator very well and follow all the instructions given without knowing that they are in the trap of being manipulated.

- For a manipulator to be able to manipulate and persuade people, they should look good before them. Your way of dressing and the way you present yourself tells a lot about you. People will only take you seriously when you look good. You will be able to earn their trust easily. People are normally impressed by people who dress nicely, who are well kept and also who have manners. They will easily like them and listen to them and in the process trust them. Once trust kicks in, the manipulators are able to easily persuade them as well as influence them in the direction that they want.

- When you are conversant about psychology, you will be able to read people's minds. You will be able to know how they feel, how they will react to certain things and also their mood. Knowing all this will be of great help in ensuring that you use their weaknesses to your advantage. You will be able to manipulate them without their knowledge.

CHAPTER 13:

The Best Techniques of Persuasion

From the previous chapter, we have already gathered what manipulation is and how best you may use manipulation to your advantage. The chapter was keen enough to take us through the facets of manipulation. This chapter, however, focuses its radar on the art of persuasion.

Before we indulge further into the major facets of persuasion, we will first have to comprehend the meaning of persuasion. Persuasion refers to the psychological influence which affects the choice that an individual ought to make. With persuasion, an individual is often inclined to make you buy his or her school of thought in a bid to change your thought process. In order for one to effectively achieve persuasion, there are a number of things that need to be put in mind. When we are able to go beyond the natural human framework and get a grasp of what moves others, then you are in a position to achieve effective persuasion. This is because you are aware of the pressure points and how best to manipulate them.

When exploiting the art of persuasion, there are various pointers that can come in handy. These are:

Mimicking

As human beings of reason, we tend to vary from one individual to another. The diversity of this is what makes us appear in the discrepancy of others. Owing to this particular fact, you will find that as individuals, we are more drawn to be warm and welcoming to those people who exhibit the same characteristics as us. It could be a physical trait or just the way an individual carries themselves out. This type of technique is said to elicit positive feelings that go a mile when it comes to persuasion. When an individual has the feelings of liking towards someone, he or she is in a position to be swayed by your influence.

In a bid to elaborate on this particular type of technique, we are going to employ the use of this scenario. In the hotel industry, especially in the most advanced and high-end ones, you will find that the allocation of a waiter is dependent on the customer. High-end hotels in the industry have high customer feedback and thus they tend to treat their clients in a manner that suggests so. A client, for instance, would be allocated a particular type of waiter who matches their description. For instance, French waiters are renowned for their exquisite service. Putting the client first is at the top of the list when it comes to this particular field. Many professionals have succeeded in this area owing to the manner in which they treated clients. This is because of the clients re the main source of business. Putting the client into consideration goes a notch higher to even saying the exact words that the client has said. With this, they are able to gather that you have aptly decoded what they meant.

In order to accurately achieve this particular technique, an individual ought to do a number of things. First, he or she may consider doing in-depth research into the particular field of the question in order to see to it that what is required of them is met. Before you are able to achieve persuasion by the use of this technique, one ought to be well versed with the individual that he or she ought to persuade. This type of expertise should be keen enough to make sure that it elicits major points that may come in handy during the process of persuasion.

Social Proof

When it comes to persuasion, social proof has repeatedly proven its dominance. Before we go deeper into the technique, we first need to gather the meaning of social proof. Social proof refers to the process by which an individual's feelings and thought process are affected by the way other people have reacted to the same issue. When it comes to social influence. An individual who is the persuader, draw his or her basis from the acts that others have engaged in time and again. It could be the norm. With human beings, the danger that occurs is the feeling of wanting to be associated with a group of people. Human beings want to accrue a sense of belonging either to a group of people or to a particular act and this is what puts them at a higher risk of being influenced easily.

Employing social proof when persuading an individual will mean that you have a basis of a norm that has been used repeatedly by the people whom we consider to be in the same class. This basis must be something that most people engage in and not a few numbers. Take, for instance, there are newbies in the estate who are looking for service providers. This newbie would first be inclined to know what other people in the estate are using. Although they might not settle on the same option as the rest of the estate, this will be somewhat a buildup on to what choice they may choose to settle upon. Rather they may end up embracing what others have used. With this technique, the trick lies whereby you ought to create a distinction in the manner in which an individual sees himself or herself as per against others. You will only achieve persuasion by convincing this individual that the desired option is one that has been embraced by a large group of individuals.

Reciprocity

When it comes to this type of technique, one needs to understand that a good deed was done to another individual no matter how remote, tends to go a long way. From the wording of it, reciprocity refers to the process by which an individual is able to respond to a good deed by performing a good deed in return. With this type of technique, we will find that most people fail to notice at its onset not until you are obligated to return the favor. In the world today, it is almost as rare as the sun rising from the west as it is to find someone who will extend feelings of warmness and care towards you. Save the people whom we are closely related, we tend to feel differently when an individual who is not even in your circle of friendship extends warm-hearted feelings.

The feeling of obligation arises as a result of being extended a good deed by an individual. This is the result of being extended with feelings of warmness. At this point, you are in a position to persuade the individual in the manner that you wish. This is because he or she would be obliged to follow in the direction of the wind. It should be noted that this particular type of technique ought to be time cautious. This is because the implication of reciprocity does not last forever. There are limits to this timeline and one should be cautious enough to make sure that these limits are not exploited. With the passing of more time, it weakens the wave of reciprocity.

In order to achieve this particular type of technique, an individual ought to play in the tone of offers and obligations. If your offer is worth it, then it raises an obligation effect on the other hand. Thus creating a win situation.

Consistency and Commitment

This type of technique is wired on an already formed perception. An individual is in a position to settle on a particular choice. The choice that this individual picks would be pegged on him or her for as far as they go. From the wording of it, consistency and commitment refer to the fact that an individual is in a position to make a choice and stick to it with sheer determination and perseverance. When it comes to persuasion, not all techniques may work and you may find that you hit rock bottom once or twice in your venture. When this happens, it is not advisable to give up. Consistency is what builds our character in almost every facet in life. This type of technique is vast in a manner that cuts across various fields not limited to the field of education and business. The first approach to an individual for purposes of convincing them may or may not end up in a manner that you wish. The first approach is often one that is characterized by rejection and in some cases mental torture. The best way to respond to this type of instance is by not giving up. The second encounter of individuals who first rejected your idea will see to it that you have an audience who understands what you are talking about.

The talk of consistency and commitment is one that does not go down the throat easily. This is because these are the most subtle facets to embrace because they tend to take a toll on an individual. You can imagine getting rejected severally. In order to achieve commitment, an individual ought to operate in a manner that is relentless.

Speed - Reading People

A step by step guide to understand how to analyze people. Learn body language secrets and the art of manipulate people through this workbook

Benedict Spot

CHAPTER 1:

How to Understand in Advance the Character of a Person

Research by MIT Media lab on negotiations conducted a study. In it, they found that, through careful study of a person's body language, and without a word of context, they came up with an exciting find. They were able to access with an 87% accuracy on the outcome of the negotiation, which they ran from telephone sales calls and business pitches.

Reading body language to understand in advance the character of a person and then know how to persuade them went beyond just looking at their body language as you communicate. In *The Silent Language of Leaders*, Carol Goman, a body language specialist, wrote about her research. In it, she identified ways in which we could accurately learn of another person's character. How they speak gives us a hint into their nature, and thus, knows how we could manipulate them.

Context: ignoring context if often one way in which we read body language wrong, for example, crossing hands if often seen as a sign being closed up. But, this can be inaccurate when the weather is cold.

Single reading: single reading was another way we made errors. Instead, Goman called for us to read body language in clusters. We needed to look beyond a single indicator to accurately judge a person's character and understand them in advance.

Baseline: here, you need to understand if a person always acted as they did when you or if they were acting out of character. A person acting out of style required you to be entirely keen on their other moves, as they could have hidden motives.

Blinding Your Biases: we all have biases and knowing them was vital in then reading people. Gorman said that liking/not liking a person, or whether or not we found them attractive, all affected us. Thus, knowing this was critical in helping you assess a person.

In another study, a personality psychologist at Texas University, Sam Gosling, stated that, unlike what we learned, first impressions were helpful to us. However, rather than sit on them as truths, we needed to update them. Thus, when you meet someone, take a moment. Trying to understand their intentions on the first meeting was useful, but you needed to be constantly monitoring the changes in their bodies. This understanding allows you to know how you will go about manipulating them to get what you wanted.

Sam went on to say that we needed to also pay attention to what he called identity claims. The identity claims said all we needed about what we wanted our goals, our attitudes, values, and many more. Therefore, someone wearing certain clothes, for example, would give you a peep into what message they wanted to pass. Again, to accurately gauge their character, and therefore, their intention, how they dressed and wore ornaments spoke of this. It was a statement that people used to display that they wanted others to know them, according to Sam.

Pennebaker, a researcher, also found that when telling the truth, most people tended to use 'I' a lot, while people lying would try to distance themselves by shying away from 'I,' as they were psychologically putting a distance between themselves and the lie. They also tended to avoid complicated language, as this would increase the likelihood of them stumbling and getting caught out on the lie.

But as we learned from the first study in this chapter, for a more accurate assessment, we need to cluster these signs. Various studies prove that it is possible to accurately read a person's body language and know their character if you do a close reading.

CHAPTER 2:

Body Language; How Important is it and What Can We Learn?

Body language is a vital communication tool.

To accurately read a person, we need body language understanding. This reading allows us to look at intentions and their character, thus, you know how you will go about the interactions so that you get what you want. We touched on this revelation in the previous chapter, where researchers and psychologists let us in on the secrets that our bodies hold beyond our control.

While we can still control the movements that we were conscious of, there is still plenty that our bodies do that we cannot control. To understand this was to become better at reading body language and expertise interact with the person. Every action that we did during a conversation matters. No matter how innocuous it seemed, it let the other person a little deeper into who we were and what our intentions were. That, of course, as if they paid attention to these social cues themselves, and whether they understood the complexities of context and cluster reading, as well as being aware of how their biases affected them.

We transfer information through body language, and body language has two angles to it.

Decoding - decoding is your ability to interpret other people's body language. You need to decode their emotions, intention, and personality or character for their body language to have a meaning to you.

Encoding - this is how we control how we send signals to others. Encoding is what controls how we make first impressions and how we interact with others to get them to like us. To encode your messages for a better social impact, you need to know yourself well.

The Role of Body Language in Communication

Having looked briefly, at what body language entails, here, we look at the functions of body language. According to body language experts, body language is vital in communication in the following ways;

Giving Cues

Regulating is where we use body language to keep the conversation going and ensuring that it is per social norms. In a social setting, there will often be indicators that we give and receive that gives us room to speak.

Conflicting/ Word and Action Do not match.

Conflicting is when your body language is inconsistent with your words. You say you are comfortable and relaxed, but keep fidgeting with your phone, or keep shuffling your feet. Conflicting reveals what we may not be confident to express through words.

Using It In Place of Words

You can substitute words with body language. Replacing is where we use body language in situations where we cannot talk. Substitution is especially useful to us when we are in public or want to keep our intentions hidden from another person within earshot.

Giving Meat to What We Say/Enhancing

Complementing is where we use body language to add to what we are saying. We might gesture, for example, when we are talking about something passionately, or describing something that had an impact on us mentally. Complementing helps to strengthen what we are saying and lends credence to what we are saying. We will often use this to help the other party visualize what we are talking about. More often, we use it when we want or need to be descriptive.

Giving Direction

As with complementing, giving direction, or repeating, it also adds to what we are saying. However, unlike complementing, repeating is something that we do in basic conversation. You might say 'pass me the salt,' as you point to the salt shaker, for example. Repeating, rather than create emphasis as with complementing, acts as a direction to the person you are talking with.

While the above example makes it seem as though our body language operates in this bright cut patterns that we have described above, there are often overlaps. Context is also essential if we are to have an accurate assessment of another person's way of thinking. Thus, how we can use that to control them then to do what we want.

Information From Body Language

People's body language can lead us into their state of mental being. It also helps us gauge how they will respond to what we will tell them. Besides, it gives us clues to how they want us to think.

Interest

Standing close to or a distance away from someone can tell you a lot about whether someone likes or does not like you. Again, context is critical. Someone might stand close to you because there is little room to maneuver. Or they might stand further from you because they value their personal space or are introverted.

Intention

Someone mimicking how you move or using words that you use is someone that is trying to get you to trust and be comfortable around them. Take care of this as many cons use this move to get you to relax around.

You could use this move to help yourself relax around people if you want to become better at persuading them to see your point of view. However, let it flow and come naturally, as you will come off as creepy when you force it. This act then means that you need to take time to practice how to mimic effortlessly.

Someone who is flirting with you will also display certain traits. These traits will show you their sexual intentions. They include; a strong, yet delicate eye contact, or speaking in a lower-pitched voice. These are reliable indicators of physiological arousal.

Character/Personality

Body language provides us with a look into how a person's character is. A person who is sitting with an open posture, for example, might be a free, extroverted person.

Someone who is easily anxious and non-confrontational might have low self-esteem, for example. Someone maintaining steady eye contact might be trying to get your attention to misdirect you so that they may manipulate you.

CHAPTER 3:

Know Yourself Well To Understand Others

How well do you understand your body language? How well do you know of your reaction to factors, both internal and external?

Learning how to read another person's body language down to the finer details would be useless if you would not know how you come across yourself. Your attempt to persuade another person to your side would be inconsequential if you did not know how you are presenting yourself. You need to be aware of; the pitch of your voice, what are your arms saying, your eyes, and your facial expressions. Whatever you put out, is what determines how others pick up your message.

How to Know Yourself Better

Identify Your Personality

To be able to work on your general body posture, you first need to identify your personality. If you want to be more charismatic and are introverted, jumping right into trying to appear more outgoing might come off as you faking it. If you are extroverted and want to be charismatic, you need to know if you exude confidence or talk a lot.

Identifying your personality is critical as it gives you a gauge of what you desire and what you do not. If you are not very outgoing, then becoming outgoing just for the sake of it will work against you.

Body Posture

Stand upright and try to be more relaxed if you are going to want to come off as confident and approachable. Unnatural slouched shoulders make you look less confident and unapproachable. When you speak to someone lean in a little to show that, you are interested in what they are saying. If you can help it, do not cross your arms. Let the other person get comfortable with you, and trust you.

Be Flexible When Communicating

When you put a point across, and the other person does not seem to be receptive to the idea, learn how to change your body language. You could change the style of delivery to convince them to see your point of view too.

Practice Facial Expression

Facial expression will often have a way of backing or taking away the punch from what we are saying. Practice this on the mirror in different scenarios. Look at how you express yourself when you are trying to convince, or when you are flirting, or when you are trying to be more confident. Refine them accordingly so that you have a better chance of convincing the other person of your point of view. Learning how to read others is an art, so is learning how to understand yourself. To read others better, you need to read yourself almost flawlessly.

Intention

Your intention guides how you align your body language to what you are saying. This book teaches you to persuade. Therefore, you need to learn how your body language will help you convince another person.

When speaking to someone else, for example, you can nod your head subtlety as you make your point. Take tab of their language and see how you can then use it to create a bond between the two of you so that they can grow to trust you.

Gestures

Using gestures when you make a point makes you come off as more charismatic and thus, will make you more trustworthy. Make use of your arms when you make a point. Use it especially, to bring out your energy and emotions to the issue you are raising. Gestures make people grow more comfortable around you.

Once you understand the above, you will find that getting to manipulate and influence people becomes more manageable, since you use your knowledge of yourself to read them and act accordingly. You will read people well this way and analyze them with startling accuracy once you know yourself well.

CHAPTER 4:

Body Language: Body Parts (The Movements and Postures That Transmit Messages)

While we have touched on a few here and there, knowing how people communicate with various movements of their body parts will deliver a lot about them. You will decipher more about a person's personality and character, as well as their intention through how they move around. It includes how they move parts of their body around, and how they generally place themselves.

Body language has two major parts: Kinesics and proxemics. Kinesics is how someone moves their body or parts of their body. Proxemics, on the other hand, is the distance between bodies and what they signify. When you become a skilled observer, you will have a reasonably accurate glimpse into what someone is thinking. That way, you can then manipulate them better.

Kinesics

Kinesics refers to the movements of body parts, which someone can use to reinforce what they are saying, or can reveal what someone is trying to hide. This way, you gain an advantage that you can use to read their minds and make your move to persuade and influence them.

They include

Body Posture - closed/open arms, slumped shoulders, etc

Body posture is basically, how someone places their body. In body language, there are two types; closed and open body postures.

A closed body posture will typically mean that the person has his hands folded across his chest. They will cross their legs and face away from the person talking to them. Some people have slumped shoulders and curved backs.

This closed body posture often communicates either that the person is uncomfortable or not interested in what you are saying. When someone has slumped shoulders and a curved back, they may be struggling with confidence, or have a lot going through their mind and feel the weight weighing them down.

An open body posture, on the other hand, communicates interest and a desire to be approached and engaged. This posture will mean that the person is welcome to a conversation and will be receptive to your desire to speak with them.

When someone has an upright standing posture, they are likely more confident and happier. These people may be optimistic.

Mirroring

Mirroring is the act where you match your body movements with the other person so that you create a synchronic situation that helps establish a bond between people. Mirroring, also called mimicry helps build trust, even when the person you are mirroring does not realize it.

While it sounds creepy, when you do it naturally, and with the right intention - to understand the other person better, it will help you read into what the other person is not saying.

Mirroring can take many forms. If the person you are talking to folds their arms, for example, it could be a sign that they are getting uncomfortable. However, you can copy them so that they become more at ease as they take it that they can trust you. Alternatively, when they lean forward, it shows that they are interested in the conversation. Lean forward too. You could also lean forward as a cue for the other person to lean in. Leaning helps, you learn more about them to that, you can then read their mind and learn how you can persuade them.

You can mimick with words too. Take a keen interest in the words that the other person frequently. Then, begin to use them sparingly through the conversation. Subconsciously, the other person will start to settle in your presence. This ease gives you room to analyze them and know how you can then approach them to persuade them of your point.

Facial Expressions

Facial expressions are other very revealing body movements. Dr. Paul Ekman, a researcher, found that we use seven different micro-expressions that reveal the bigger picture; surprise, fear, disgust, anger, contempt, sadness, and happiness. These micro-expressions determined how to read well if someone was faking.

A genuine smile, for example, should involve various muscles on the face; cheeks, lips, and the eye muscles. A genuine smile will spread across the whole look. Keep note of that when someone smiles at you.

Proxemics

Proxemics is the study of how we relate to personal space. The thing with proxemics is that it is different from cultures and varies from individual to individual.

However, there is a little that we can learn from proxemics.

Close Distance - Interest

There is a close distance called the close range. We have this kind of distance with people that we are close with and trust. Often, entering into this distance with someone you are not close with is disturbing and creepy in many cultures and with many people. So, to avoid turning off the other person, keep a safe distance. Ensure that you are close enough, but not too close to make them uncomfortable and closeout to your interactions. Someone might also get close to you if they are interested in you. The person might not get too close to you, but they will get close enough to you to pass a message. If a person is trying to catch your attention, for example, they will get into your personal space but not get into the close distance. However, as we have learned, context is vital. Use this measure with other indicators, as someone might stand close to you because that is the appropriate distance in their culture, or that is just how they view space.

Social Distance - Impersonal/Formal

Social Distance is the distance we maintain with people such as business associates, people we are professional around. We often use social distance for co-workers who we are not well acquainted with or business associates.

The distance also refers to tilt. If one person sits in a position where they appear to look down on the other person, it may mean that they want to come across as authoritative.

Pubic Distance - Respectability

This distance happens in a situation where you cannot get close to the other person because of the many limiting factors. At such a range, arm movement and gestures become critical. When in public, make a point of using head movement to pass your point, especially when you speak to a crowd. These body movements allow them to bond with you despite the distance. Look at some of the most admired public speakers. You will notice that they use hand movements and gestures a lot, as well as head movement and exaggerated facial expressions.

Our body language speaks in ways that we should take time to understand. But, as we have said, always use them in context for better analysis of the other person.

CHAPTER 5:

Body Language in Men and Women -What Are All Those Gestures That Hide Unspoken Words

B ody language plays a significant role in our day-to-day communication. It refers to nonverbal gestures and signals that both men and women use to express emotions with their bodies without saying a word. Our body gestures and facial expression speak volumes about what we do not say when it comes to conveying information. Experts suggest that more than half of all communication is accounted for by our body language. Body language and learning how to interpret it is essential. While interpreting body language, it is vital to understand the context of the conversation and be attentive to any other cues. You should also not draw your conclusion by focusing on a single action, but you should look at signals as a group so that you can pull the right conclusion.

Facial expressions

The way we express our faces conveys a lot of information to others. You may say that you are well and good, but depending on the look on your face, some will be able to tell that you are not ok.

People can trust or distrust what you are saying based on the look on your face

- **Happiness or approval** is usually indicated by a smile, while a frowning face will express sadness and disapproval.
- **A slight smile and a slight raise** of the eyebrows is a sign of being trustworthy, because it is a show of confidence and being friendly.
- **Intelligence** is associated with people who are joyful and have a smiling expression, more prominent noses, and narrower faces, rather than those with angry expressions.

The eyes

The eyes are the windows to the soul because their movements can reveal the feelings and thoughts of a person during a conversation. Some things that you should look out for in the eyes are dilation of the pupil, blinking of the eyes, and whether a person averts their gaze or makes direct eye conduct.

- **Eye conduct** – if a person maintains direct eye conduct during a conversation, it shows that they are attentive and interested. However, a prolonged gaze is threatening and can be an attempt to control you. If a person frequently breaks wye conduct and keep on look away, it shows that they are uncomfortable, distracted, or trying to hide their real feeling and motives.
- **Blinking** – blinking should be natural. If a person blinks too rapidly that it is natural, it is a sign that they are uncomfortable or distressed. Someone may try to control their blinking intentionally to hide their true feelings purposely, so you should be careful to notice the

infrequent blinking of the eyes. When blinking is accompanied by touching the mouth, eyes, and face, it is an indication that the person is lying.

- **Pupil size** – sometimes, emotions or feelings come with some changes in the size of the pupil. When the eyes are highly dilated, it is maybe an indication that someone is aroused or interested. It also shows a favorable response.
- **Looking down** –this indicates that the person is submissive or nervous.
- **Glancing** – it expresses a desire for something. Glancing at a person means that you desire to talk to them or be with them, while glancing at the door may indicate that the person wants to leave.
- **Looking upward and to the right** – it is a sign that someone is telling a lie. When people are trying to concoct a story using their imagination, they look that way.
- **Looking up and to the left** – it is a sign that the person is speaking the truth. People look that way when they are trying to recall an actual memory.

The mouth

Someone who keeps can express insecurity, fear, or worry on chewing the bottom lip. Some may cover the mouth to cough or yawn politely, but it can also be a way of covering up a frown of expressing disapproval. You should watch out genuine smiles that show happiness, and false smiles meant to express cynicism or sarcasm. A genuine smile engages the whole face, while a false one is done with the mouth alone.

- **Pursed lips** – when a person tightens the lips, it is an indication of distrust, distaste or disapproval.
- **Biting the lip** - this is a sign of being stressed, worried, or anxious.
- Covering the mouth – a person may try to hide emotional reactions such as smirks or smiles by covering their mouths.
- **Turning the mouth up or down** - outright grimace, sadness or disapproval is expressed with the mouth slightly turned down. When the mouth is turned up slightly, it may be a show of feeling optimistic or happy.
- **A fake smile** – it uses the mouth only. It tries to show approval or pleasure, but it is a clear sign that the person is feeling otherwise.
- **A genuine smile** – it engages the whole face. It is an indication of happiness and approval and shows that the person is thoroughly enjoying your company.
- **Half-smile** – engages one side of the mouth, and it is used to express uncertainty, sarcasm, grimace, or cynicism.

\\

Arms and Legs

- **Crossed arms** – this might be a sign that someone is closed-off, defensive or self-protective.
- **Hands-on the hip** – when someone stands with their hands on the hip, it may show that they are in control or that they are ready. This can also be a sign of someone who is aggressive.
- **Hands clasped behind the back** – it is a sign that someone is feeling angry, anxious, or bored.

- **Fidgeting or tapping fingers rapidly** - is expresses frustration, impatience, or boredom.
- **Crossed legs** – indicates the need for privacy, dislike, discomfort or feeling closed-off

Posture

- **Open posture** – the trunk of the body is kept exposed and accessible, and it shows willingness, friendliness, and being free with others.
- **Closed posture** – the legs and the harms are kept crossed, and the body trunk is often hidden by the person hunching forward. It shows that someone is being anxious, unfriendly and hostile.

Proximity

The distance a person keeps from you during a conversation speaks volumes.

- **Standing or sitting close** – it is a good sign of rapport. It shows that the other person views you favorably. However, if a person steps into your personal space and begins to touch you, it shows that they are trying to control you.
- **Backing up or moving away** - when you move closer and the other person steps backward it is an indicator that there is no mutual connection.

CHAPTER 6:

How to Decipher
Verbal Communication

To fully understand and decode the message in the other person's words, there are some things about verbal communication that you should master. This is regardless of whether you are engaging in face-to-face or written communication.

Be an active listener

To master the art of active listening, you must be able to listen beyond the words being spoken. This means that you listen, aiming to decipher and understand the message being communicated. A lot of people listen with the wrong motive and end up missing what the other person is saying. Instead of listening to decipher the other person's point of view, they listen while thinking about how they will respond. They fail to concentrate on what the speaker is saying and miss the point.

When you listen carefully and actively, you can answer thoughtfully, taking into account the other person's perceptions, views, and opinions. The rule of thumb should always be to listen more and talk less. But how do you become an active listener? Here is how:

1. **Pay attention**

   You should learn to give others full attention when they are speaking:

   - Maintain eye contact by looking at the speaker directly while they share their side of the story.
   - While the other person is talking, don't try to think about how you will reply or respond.
   - Pay attention to the speaker's body language and interpret it
   - Avoid any distraction by anything else that is going on around you

2. **Show your interest in what the other person is saying.**

   - Encourage the speaker by nodding your head and using other prompts like "yep," "uh-huh," and so on.
   - Highlight your engagement using your body language, such as maintaining an open posture, nodding your heads, and smiling.

3. Clarify your understanding

Clarify how you have understood the speaker's message with them. As you do that, keep your beliefs and judgments out of the way.

- Paraphrase and summarize as a way of reflecting on what you have heard. Do this periodically as the conversation goes on to help you understand better. It is also a great way to help the other person feel that you are listening. For example, "if I got you clearly, you said that ...." Or "correct me if I'm wrong, but my understanding of that is ..."

- Ask non-judgmental questions to seek clarification and ensure that you grasp everything.

- When you are not sure of what the speaker says or means, admit.

- If it will help, ask the person to repeat what they said

- Ask for elaborative examples

- Accept to be corrected in the event where you get what the speaker said wrongly.

4. Don't redirect or interrupt the conversation

When you interrupt another person's speech, you reduce your time for understanding the message, besides irritating the speaker.

- Do not interject unnecessarily, when the other person is speaking. Let them finish their part, and don't say anything unless the speaker has driven home the point they are trying to make.

- Don't go outside the topic or try to divert the conversation based on your beliefs, views, or opinions.

5. **Provide a suitable response**
   - When you make a response, try to be honest. Don't attack or make the other person feel bad. Doing so is immature and unhelpful.
   - If you want to give your views, perceptions, or opinions, do so in a polite manner.

6. **Avoid the common enemies of active listening**. They include:
   - Arguing
   - False assumptions which come as a result of jumping into conclusion
   - Losing concentration
   - Trying to quickly formulate a response before the other person finishes making their point.

Be empathetic

This means that you can understand and identify with other person's emotions by imaging yourself in their shoes or positions. When you have the ability to know how others feel, it can help you understand them when they communicate. You will also be able to convey your ideas and thoughts sensibly and care for other peoples' feelings.

If you want to understand other people's verbal communication, take these concrete steps to develop empathy.

- Put yourself in the other person's position. Think of the time when you experienced the same feelings/ emotions which the speaker is experiencing. It doesn't have to be precisely the same, but you can think of a related situation.

- Think of how you would feel if someone keeps on interrupting you before you make your point. That way, you will learn to let others talk without interrupting them.
- Observe your colleagues well as they speak and try to grasp the feelings or emotions they are communicating through the words.
- If you notice that your colleague is conversing emotionally, do not despise or ignore them. Understand it and address it. Give them time to cool down.
- Seek to understand, but not to judge. For instance, when your colleague seems disinterested and cold at first, you may capture a feeling of being annoyed with them. But after you learn that they have a problem of being socially anxious, you will be more sympathetic and give them time to relax and make their point.
- Don't seek to corner your colleague, or engage yourself in a conversation with the mentality of winning it. Learn to regulate your voice so that you can communicate your empathy by being sincere and keeping your body language open.

Seek to understand first

If you want the other person to understand you, seek to understand them first. Don't try to force your ideas, thoughts, perceptions, or opinions on others. To do that is to approach a conversation with a closed mind, and it will only result in unnecessary arguments. The best way to decipher verbal communication is to listen and understand the beliefs, thoughts, and perspectives of the other person so that you can know why they hold them. You do not have to agree with them, but at least you will understand why they think the way they think.

Therefore, learning to listen actively, being empathetic, and mastering the art of understanding others first, is the master key to deciphering any form of verbal communication. Running into conclusions will only result in assumptions and confusion, and you will end up missing the point the other person is attempting to make.

CHAPTER 7:

The Meaning of the Words

Words are an expression of an individual's thoughts and emotions. No matter how much someone tries to hide what is in their mind, their words will always betray them in one way or another. The world of dark psychology employs this technique to get into people's minds and perform wonders. When it comes to the meaning of words, dark psychology does not pay attention to the literal meaning of those words; it is never related to meanings found in the dictionary. What someone will look for is the actual meaning coming from within the speaker; what is really in their mind. The following combination of factors will help you decipher the actual meaning in the words of the target.

Pitch

This is the pitch in the speaker's speech. Do they say some words with a high voice and others with a low one? The tone with which words are said speaks volumes about the feelings and thoughts of an individual. Let us look at the following example; a politician and presenter are having a chat on national television.

POLITICIAN: the citizens must be excited that I am selling my manifestos here today.

PRESENTER: oh yeah? It is expected.

POLITICIAN: My social media is flooding with messages of goodwill (low); my opponents must see that (high).

PRESENTER: but first let us hear what you have in store for the people.

POLITICIAN: most of them already know my agendas, but I will repeat it anyway.

PRESENTER: You cannot be so sure, sir. It is your first time on-air; this is a good opportunity to boost your popularity (low).

POLITICIAN: (whispering) very well, I did not know I am not known.

PRESENTER: hey, just not enough (low).

(The politician sighs)

From this dialogue, we see that the politician is trying hard to make the presenter believe that he is popular while he is not. He cunningly tries to avoid addressing the issues directly by using general words like 'agendas' and 'manifestos'. He manipulates his way into the presenter's mind and finds the truth-he is not all that popular. The use of the words 'citizens' 'the people' and 'social media' indicate that the politician is targeting popularity. We can also get to read the politician's mind from the pitch in his voice. He says his social media pages are flooding with messages of goodwill with a low voice, an indication that he desperately needs the fame he is talking about. The low voice means the 'flooding' is a mere exaggeration. The second part of that statement is more of a threat directed at his opponents, some sort of propaganda, 'my opponents must see'. The use of the word 'must' about his opponents tells us that he is just bluffing. He has no control over what his opponents should or should not do whatsoever.

Pick Cues

Sometimes the speaker does not bring out their thoughts using the right words. They will use a variety of synonyms and other techniques to deliberately mislead the listener. Dark psychologists will pick these cues from the words spoken and use them to accurately read the speaker's mind. Let us look at the following examples.

"After the wedding, I patiently waited in the queue until I got served."

The clue here is the word 'patiently'. This statement means the speaker was not only hungry but they also had no alternative other than following the long queue to the end. It says a lot about their financial position as well as the significance of that event to them. This information can be used to press the right buttons if the person is to be manipulated into doing something they would otherwise not agree to easily. You could promise such a person plenty of food or financial assistance as a way of winning them. Here is another practical example:

"Not that I'm afraid of heights, I just don't trust our engineers."

These are the words of someone that is afraid of heights but finds a good excuse to cover it up. The mention of the word 'afraid' is enough evidence of the underlying fear. This fact is reinforced by the kind of reason they give. Technically, all buildings have not been built by one person and unless it is condemned, then there is no cause for alarm. And does it mean the person will never enter a high-story building? Not, the bottom line here is the person is afraid of heights. You can easily use this weakness on their part to manipulate them.

The trick when it comes to picking cues is no analyzing every word spoken by someone in a sentence. Relate every word with the previous and subsequent one to get its meaning and context. This will help you to identify misplaced words that will serve as cues. The cues will, in turn, put you in a better position to read someone's mind quite easily.

Look out for repetitions

Words that are repeated repeatedly are something to pay attention to if you are looking to discover what is in someone's mind. It means the speaker is desperately trying to communicate their thoughts but they do so in a way that people will not understand. These words can be synonyms or related sentiments so it takes a lot of scrutinizes to identify. Look at the following three statements.
I would love to have a big car when I find a good job.

My mum would have bought an expensive dress if my neighbor's daughter's graduation was mine.

I watched an action movie with robots that built castles in the sky.

The three sentences have a consistent similarity in that they are centered on big things, luxurious ones for that matter. These things are the person's biggest fantasies. If you analyze the sentences keenly, you will notice that the words 'big', 'expensive', and 'sky' are related. They all have something to do with success. This tells us that the speaker has a strong desire to live largely. It also tells us that their current condition is nowhere near their fantasies. This intense craving for material success can be used to manipulate such an individual. Dark psychologists would listen to someone speak, not to understand them but to notice those words that person keeps emphasizing.

CHAPTER 8:

How to Pay Attention to Details

To effectively hack someone's mind, you must learn to pay attention to every single detail concerning every single word they utter and body movements. The words they use are major cues people use to express their thoughts. Body movements are just mere reinforcements for those words. Try to create a connection between every word spoken and the accompanying movement, these two could be simultaneous or separate. Learning to relate words and movements will come in handy when looking out for people that want to manipulate you. We shall study single words and movements in this chapter as a technique of paying attention to details. This will be illustrative for ease of understanding.

The link between Body Movement and Words

Prominent public speakers undergo intense training before standing before an audience to speak. Those close to figures like presidents and religious leaders will confirm to you that indeed the training can last several months or even years. The reason this happens is to ensure whatever they speak to the audience is exactly what is in their mind, whether it is the truth or just lies. However, one can still read their minds accurately despite vigorous training. The relationship between words and movements can easily sell them out; it is difficult to fake emotions throughout the speech. If someone is narrating a sad event, for example, their movements will be quite different from those associated with an exciting event. Let us analyze the following case.

"Ladies and gentlemen, we are saddened beyond the comprehension of words by the sudden and untimely demise of our brothers and sisters in the ferry that sank on Monday morning. Our gallant men in blue have been working day and night to retrieve the bodies since the tragedy happened. Unfortunately, it breaks my heart to announce to you that all has been an effort in futility. Our intelligence has revealed that the bodies have been buried deep in the murky seawaters, a situation that is complicating the process of retrieving the bodies, as we do not have sufficient equipment for such an undertaking. We require more than four tanks of oxygen for each diver; a resource that is not plenty in supply at the moment. We have also come to a logical conclusion that sending those divers to the bottom of the ocean is nothing short of putting their innocent lives at great risk. We have therefore decided to call off the operation to avoid losing more lives. I know this is not the best news for the families of the victims but it is the right thing to do. We shall hold a vigil for the victims by the sea for the next two days. It is not enough but it is the best we can do at this point, our hands are tied."

Let us analyze this speech by a government official about an ill-fated sunken ferry that claimed the lives of all its occupants. We want to try and read the speaker's mind and verify these claims. We shall be in a position to tell whether this is just another ploy to cover up for the government's unwillingness to find the remains of its deceased citizens or there is some logic in it.

"We are saddened"

We know whether this statement is genuine by observing the way the speaker says it and accompanying movements. First of all, the word 'saddened' should be mentioned with a low, dejected and troubled voice. Second, it should be accompanied by a little bow or dilation of the pupils. To emphasize it further, there ought to be a brief silence before the speaker continues.

"Beyond the comprehension of words"

This statement means that words cannot explain the feeling, so actions ought to play that role. The speaker could press their lips together or cross their arms to show despair.

"Brothers and sisters"

The look in the face of the speaker as these words come out of mouth should reveal the feeling one would have when talking about the loss of a real brother and sister. Mentioning those words would likely send shivers all over the speaker's body. The lips could tremble, the voice ought to be shaky and they could even choke in their words. If the voice is smooth and clear, then we have reason to doubt the speaker's true feelings about the victims.

"Effort in futility"

This statement implies despair. The speaker's voice should express that, especially when saying the word 'futility'.

Body movements that could be associated with this statement include crossing arms, slight bowing of the head and bringing feet together.

"Murky"

The literal meaning of this word is dark and gloomy. Regarding ocean waters, it becomes even scarier. We should pay attention to the way the speaker says this dreadful word. We expect his face to show this by looking just like it-dark and gloomy. We need to feel the pain of saying the word in his voice; is it shaky? We need to see the pain written on his face. His hands should also speak of the feeling. Are the fists clutched? Are the fingers crossed? Are the arms folded around the chest? Look for anything that will show the dreadful nature of that word.

"Logical conclusion"

The way the speaker says the word 'logical' should tell you whether the conclusion is indeed a logical one or it is just another wild claim. The amount of stress applied to the word indicates the extent of seriousness. If he says it casually, then it means he is just trying to dupe his listeners with a technical word. Also, does his explanation support the weight of the word? Is it logical that a whole country is unable to acquire enough oxygen for the exercise?

By keenly analyzing some single words used by the speaker, together with his body movements, we will be able to read his mind and ascertain the sincerity of his words. If the speaker had the intention of manipulating this audience, only those equipped with mind-reading skills will escape the snare.

CHAPTER 9:

Lies (Like Discovering a Lie, the Best Technique to Understand a Lie from Movements of Words, Or In Behavior)

Remember that time you did something without the permission of your parents. How did you feel when lying? Probably you felt unsure whether you will succeed in cheating your parents. But how do your mother or father notice that you were lying? Perhaps it is your behavior or the choice of words you undertook. Many situations force omen to rest, but one should know deceitful conduct is a vice. It will still cause chaos among your loved ones. You may succeed in lying to the court of something you had done, but that guilt and conscience will not leave you. Therefore you must be pure always like where the truth will set you free.

One aspect to check is the physical body movement. Remember that everyone experiences some uneasiness when cheating; thus, the body will tend to detach itself from that deceitful mood. These moods can be dissipated in very many ways that change your behavior. That is where some people shake and mumble when they are telling a lie. That cheating guilt will envelop them and make them shiver with the fear of being caught lying. Moreover, if you spot a whitish element in the lips, know that they are lying.

Check on their eyes. Remember that the eyes will read your heart and mind and dispel information according to your emotional state. Therefore when you lie, then there are some signs showed by the eyes. Those who blinks a lot of time while telling a story is evidence of cheating. Your eyeballs may know if you are cheating too. Sometimes your eyes may dance around your sockets when you are deceiving someone. It is like that guilt triggers to move around the sockets

Consider other body reactions to spot in a liar. These different reactions are fidgeting methods. They are objects one holds to try to hide or escape from the cheating mood. That is where some people feel nervous and look uncomfortable at your presence. Some may like to maintain a long-distance from you because they suspect if they are near, you can easily read their lies. Others would decide to play with the items available like trying to tighten a dress, touching your hair or any other piece of clothing.

Look at their change in their tone. That means the tonal variation is very significant to detect the lies. For example, you can quickly identify this change of voice of a person in normal circumstances. You will undoubtedly realize that change. Maybe in their stable mind, they talk slowly and tranquil, but at this time they speak fast and stammers. They also have an inconsistent tone, where it changes at any time. That is because they are describing imaginative events where they forget the right voice balancing.

Diagnose their chat manner when intermingling with other people. Liars would take time to think of words to fill in making a story amusing. That means that their word flow is unfortunate as they take a long time to make a sentence. You will realize how they use jargon and vocabulary to deviate your interest in what you want them to tell you. Moreover, they can chatter to make the words look meaningless, which would make you lose attention in them.

Deceivers always talk in general terms. They avoid the use of the first pronoun persona but use the general pronouns like 'they', 'them', 'him' or others. That is a way of trying to cover their involvement in that ordeal. They may even distract you with exciting news which is different from your earlier discussion. That is like trying to talk about the current crisis, politico, sports and other fascinating subjects.

Identify their inconsistency in their communication. That is one strategy used in the prisoners' dilemmas. If you are telling the truth, then you should respond to the same answer even when asked later. However ask liars the same thing they said earlier, and you will realize how they forget that sateen. Moreover, you will know how they struggle to revert thee words they said.

Their facial communication is another way that can tell you whether they are dishonest. Cheaters always show different visual expressions. That is where if these respondents are gloomy and bored if you keep investigating their honesty Others will be excited if they feel you have fallen for their trap. They still fake a moaning face to harness your sympathy. Check on their eye contact to know how they look at you. If they watch you with nervous or looks you with an uncertain attitude, see that they are lying. Moreover, they will dodge your eye contact as they feel guilty of lying.

All of their behaviors are exaggerated. Look at their smiles which they fake. Remember that smiles convey honesty, sincerity, and understanding. Real smiles typically appear naturally contracted on your muscles. However, fake smiles are consciously contracted and appear elongated on the cheeks than the genuine smiles. Look at the laughter, it is overdone, and it goes over more minutes than usual. If you are asking them maybe about reported stolen cash from a bank account which they were involved in, you will rely on their exaggerated pity. Their eyes will look you with mercy, such that you can forgive them if they are caught. Contemplate how an innocent person is usually bold and confident about what they are saying.

Pay attention to how they voice the word "No." It is a means of opposing any issue on liars. They will say no even a situation where not requiring their response. They will always jump to conclusions like "are you implicating me, do you think am the thief "? Normally, truthful people, that idea of the thief will not come to their mind as quickly as those of the guilty one. Look at where they focus their eyes when saying "no." You will realize that either they will close their eyes, look in a different direction or say it after hesitating for sometimes. Their tone in saying "no "will also appear exaggerated.

CHAPTER 10:

Truth (How to Recognize a Fact)

Honesty is the significant parameter and virtue that is recommendable. That is particularly even in the jobs and occupations where one is required to curb the corruption cases. There are times when one is needed to tell the truth. For example, in the court, you will mostly hear the judge or the jury demanding to know the truth. Truthfulness is a virtue that must be prominent in you everywhere you go. Most of the time, you will find yourself in a situation where the truth will set you free. Imagine that you are captured and tortured in a military war. What proximity of the pin would make you tell the truth? Therefore if you can be honest at least, there will be no needles been inserted in your fingertips.

Ways to Know Someone Is Telling the Truth.

Check on the facial expression when the person is telling a story. They usually will show a confident face. Can you differentiate that person who is shy and sure, one aspect you can look in both of them is their face? They know what they are saying is true and will want you to show it even with their face. In every mood of the story, they will express every feeling. In every narration, there is a mixed reaction. There is that point in the story where it was joyous, and then the situation changed when there were terrible outcomes. Therefore the narrator will express all the moods with the facial manifestation. If it were a liar involved, he or she would forget to input the necessary expression on the face.

Look at how they express their point of the statement. The honest speak with clarity and are precise. There is no space for ambiguity as those characters explain all details perfectly. Their words seem to flow well as they are describing how a situation transpired. If they were lying, then you ought to note some hesitation in their statements. That is where they are looking for the word to fill the puzzle. There is no exaggeration, but they speak on a real basis. The tone used in that point is consistent. That would be unlikely for anyone who is lying as they would stress the major points they want to be heard and lower the tone on their unwanted details.

Recognize how steady their breath is. The falsifiers tend to cheat and will feel guilty of the wrong they are saying. That guilt is dissipated with their breathing problems. You can know even when they are panicking as they breathe inconsistently. They may start transpiring slowly than that rhythm changes and you realties how they began much breathing fast. A genuine person will breathe consistently at the same rhythm when they thought the conversation person will still look at you at some points. If the individual fails to see you or maintain much eye contact, know that they are lying.

The truth is something that you own and should not be deviated; however, many times, you are asked of a story. Look at the techniques most investigators use, which is the prisoners' dilemma. That is where the suspects are locked in different rooms. Each culprit is also told to narrate their side of the story. What will most detectives look like the divergence and the correction of the story? If the suspects seem to contradict, then one of them lying. If they say the same thing, then they are hones, or they had planned a lie. It is upon you, the detective to use all the instruments sat your disposal to ensure that the information being said is true. Their knowledge is still consistent as they do not deviate even if asked five or ten years to come. There is no way you can forget an event, but you can remember what you said earlier. If then you are lying, you will contradict your earlier spoken words.

Speaking in completes sentence is what define you an honest guy, liars will try to make their statement a puzzle that you may find hard understanding. Reliable individuals will speak in long sentences with clarity. You will not find any ambiguity in the report. What you will identify in their phrases is the completeness of the sentence structure. You will not find any jargon and vocabulary in their comments.

Trust in your instincts when inquiring for information. These are the inner conscience that makes you sensitize something. If you feel something terrible will happens, then it might occur, which is a result of your instincts. It is like the first impression that you will generate from a person. If you feel that this person is telling the truth, then they must be accurate, but if you think otherwise take caution.

The body motions of these people are other determinates. Remember that when you are honest, you are very confident. Therefore you do not expect to see somebody covering their mouth, head, chest or throat to be truthful. The posture of your body will also tell if you are bending one side and sitting with closed legs as if you are hiding something important. Some may prefer a far distance from you as they feel insecure about your presence. Their cheating nature makes them feel vulnerable to stay close to you.

Honesties do not like blaming others for their mistakes. They will, however, blame themselves. They are ready to face the consequences and feel that they are responsible for a disdainful act. They trust their inner feelings which they know may result in the wrong actions taken. Contrary to them, there are the cons and the fraudsters who like blaming others on their misfortunes they do not want to be caught as they fear the penalties. Note how those persons drag somebody else name in the story. Identify how also they will try to justify themselves.

Perhaps you have taken an oath or a vow on a wedding aisle. How did you feel when you made some unconditional promises? You must have felt happy and pressured not to break any promise. If you want an honest individual note how they swear before narrating the ordeal. Yes, the cheaters will also declare, but the guilt will be drawn on their faces; however much they hate. People reeling the truth usually like swearing as they stress their integrity.

CHAPTER 11:

Techniques and Practical Methods to Actively Analyze People

For you to understand the personality of a person, you need to examine them. You need to dig deep into their life so that you can know the kind of person you are dealing with. For you to understand how to treat them, you need to go the extra mile. You need to know how you can provoke them and whether they are hostile when they are subject to certain situations. You need to be in a position that you can tell what is happening when you look at them. The way they communicate should say to you more about them. That is the reason you should pay attention to everything that is happening in their life. When you analyze someone, you will get to know what they like and what they dislike. There are numerous ways that you need to consider that will help you to analyze a person. They include and not limited to;

How to Ask the Right Questions

When you need to ask the right question, it means that you need a clear answer from someone. You have to be discreet so that you will avoid a lot of complications. When you complicate things, you will not get the right information that you require from someone. That means that if you do not get the correct information, you will not understand them. Meaning you will not achieve your goal, which is to analyze them. Avoid rhetorical questions because that will not make you get the answer that you need. It might piss off the person, and they fail to let their guard down. Asking a rhetorical question means that you are forcing them to give you a specific answer that you need. The answer may be different from what you need to know. But because you have forced them to say that they will say it to please you. That will get you nowhere since you designed the answer you need and it may not be the real thing. When you are asking the question, make sure you do that in a friendly way. Rightly asking a query will not make the person defensive, and they will be comfortable to answer any question. When you demean a person, they will not be satisfied to give you honest feedback.

If you need to know someone better, do not try to set traps for them making them be on the spot. Ask a question without erecting a box around the person for them to be free to answer you. That is how you can know the kind of person you are dealing with. It will be appropriate to make an open-ended question so that the person you want to analyze will have the freedom to explain more about it. When you do not place bonds, you will give a person the time to respond appropriately in detail as well as nuance. Giving them a chance to make their choices will cause them to pour out their hearts to you. Even if you are up to something, you must avoid being direct so that the respondent will not be rigid. As you are asking the questions, you need to be as well willing to listen. Take a breather at times so that the person will not think as though you are interrogating them and refuse to give you the answers. They will not be quick to know that you are on a fact-finding mission. If you ask a question and you sense that they are uncomfortable, it is good that you rephrase it. You must be grateful when the person agrees to answer the questions so that they can feel appreciated.

When to be Aggressive

When things are tough to be a bit aggressive so that you will get the information that you need. Do that knowing that you are after your interest and you need to make the person talk. Although you will be aggressive, you need to make sure that you do your research on the person thoroughly. You need to do that politely so that the person will not get pissed off. When they are annoyed, they will not let you access anything about you, and it will get harder on you. Someone may even turn to be a stranger, and they were a friend before you got aggressive. That is the reason you should do it in the politest way possible. Give them enough space so that they will pour out all that you require to know about them. Talking too fast will make them hold some information that you may be necessary. Do not brag since that will make them think that you are not of the same level and they will not be open to you.

When to Observe the Behavior of Others

Put in mind that people behave in different ways, and each is unique. When you see the behavior of a person, you will learn more about them. Their actions will speak more about the person they are. When one is thinking that, no one is seeing them that is the time that they will be the real person they are. You need to time that moment that the person thinks they are alone and you can see the person they are. Check their habits and know what differentiates them from other people. From each observation that you are likely to make, you will have a brief thing to learn about the person. When you are figuring out the views that you have made, it is necessary that you establish whether that is the real thing. At times, you can make a conclusion that is not right, and that will give you the wrong image of the person. If you are illegal in the end that you are making, you need to improve your observation techniques so that you will not misjudge things. When you create an observation, it is time that you use your imagination to think about how that person is like. That will give you an analysis of the person they are and what is unique in them that you cannot find on anyone else.

CHAPTER 12:

How to Take Advantage of the Techniques Learned to Achieve Success and Enjoy the Esteem of Others

Y ou need to know that the methods you are using can make you successful in analyzing someone and can as well earn you respect. That is what you should aim for when you embark on the journey to investigate someone. You need to gain their esteem even though you are out on a mission. That is the reason they should not know that you are up to something. When they come to a realization that you are researching on them, they will not be comfortable with you, and they might end up disrespecting you. Be polite when you are asking the questions you have to, and you will hit your goal. When you get your target that is the moment that you will know that, you are a success. When you get, the full information that you need about the person is when you need to rest.

Here is how you need to take advantage of the techniques that you decide to put in place to analyze a person.

Knowing Yourself

When you are set on the journey to see the person you are, you will have access to your hidden wisdom. That will be so because you will behave enough space as well as time to explore that person you are. Knowing yourself better will then give you the chance to analyze the person next to you. You will explore new opportunities that you were not aware of them before. That will make you achieve great things since you are now aware of your potential. When you get to know the real person you are, you will with no doubt, be productive and with fewer efforts. You will be more inspired to do great things without having to invest much power. When you know who you are, it will be easy for you to make decisions, and you will not have to struggle to make the decision that fits you. In that way, you will attract respect from the people around you since you are a self-driven person. When you know what you want as well as who you are, that is the time that you will begin being successful and doing great things.

Truth

When you always tell the truth, it will set you free, and you do not have to remember anything you said so that you do not mess up. Once you tell a lie, you have to keep reminding it in case you are asked the same thing, and you will not contradict yourself. When you learn to speak the truth, you will with no doubt earn trust as well as respect. You will gain respect for who you are and will like to be associated with you. When you learn to tell lies, most are the times that you will fail since you will prefer to use the wrong channels of doing things. The truth will always make you win the trust of people, and you will have more connections through that. You need to know that for you to be successful, you need people to elevate you. No one will be willing to be there for you if all you can do is lie to them. When you are truthful, you will be trusted. It means that everyone will offer you an opportunity to use your potential to the benefit of all. You will be more confident, and you will not even lie to yourself, which is a good recipe for a person's downfall. You will not be betraying your thoughts as well as beliefs, and that will earn you respect from people. Telling the truth will attract people who are truthful as well.

Interpreting Personality

When you want to analyze someone, you need to explain their character so that you will know who they are. In the process, you will as well see the person you are and your preferences. When you are aware of your preferences, you will be efficient as well as productive. You will know when you are beyond your boundaries, and that will help and the extent you can go. When you are aware of that, you will improve in terms of productivity, efficiency as well as time management. When all that is in combination, there is no room for negotiations, and you will be successful in the end. When you know your personality, you will be in a position to avoid conflicts and constant fights with people. When you are not conflicting with people, be sure they will give you the respect that you deserve. Being receptive to specific situations will show the kind of character you are. It does not matter whether you are at fault or not, avoid getting into fights, and people will treat you with respect.

When you know that you are unique from the other person, and you have differences, you will embrace diversity. When you appreciate diversity, you will have a chance to explore all the possibilities that are there to lead you to success. When you understand the difference, you will attract respect from people from the diversified groups since they will feel part of you. You will have great ideas because of the many creative minds that you have brought together. The more brilliant ideas there is the likely hood that you will succeed in your missions. When you understand what your likes and dislikes are, you can make decisions based on what you prefer. When you do something out of a will, you will have good results compared to what you are being forced. You will put all the senses at work so that they can gather the collect information for you. That is when you are going to make choices based on your instincts, and that will not mislead you. You will make implementations on the decisions and you will end up being successful.

When you know your personality type, you will be in a position to see the field in which you can do better. You will know the responsibilities that you can handle thoroughly and the goals you can achieve in a given time. Understanding your personality will help you in finding out the career that fits your best. That is where you ought to invest your energy as well as resources to be successful.

Book 2:
"Dark Psychology: rewire your mind workbook"

CHAPTER 13:

Applying manipulation and mind reprogramming in different roles

As you are aware of by now, your thoughts play a major role in your choices and decision-making in everyday life. We tend to play different roles as life progresses. In this section, we look at these different roles and the way negative thinking can hold us back. Your thoughts influence your behaviors, which in turn, shape your life. So, learning to regulate negative thinking and replacing it with positive paradigms is quintessential for becoming successful. Starting from your personality and your role, you will learn about simple exercises you can use to change your negative paradigms into positive ones.

Salesperson

What is the primary goal of a salesperson? To increase sales. To do this, you must be good at networking and effectively communicating with others. Apart from that, you must also be able to influence the decisions of others. To do this, you need to have not only an acute sense of self-awareness but also an awareness of others desires. If your goal is to increase your sales, then any thinking pattern that doesn't help you attain this goal is undesirable. Perhaps you doubt your ability to sell, or maybe you believe that the customer will never make a purchase. In such a situation, attaining your goal can become extremely tricky.

To become a great salesperson, you need plenty of self-confidence. Confidence must come from within, and unless you truly believe in yourself and what you are pitching, others will have difficulty believing you. Any negative beliefs you have about yourself will effectively hinder your selling skills. If you seem meek, unsure of yourself, and fumble while talking, this won't elicit confidence. Don't let your negative thought patterns hold you back.

Exercises

Your Circle

The company you keep matters. Past a certain age, who you are and how you interact with others is usually a direct representation of the kind of people you spend most of your time with. So, take some time and think about your different circles of friends. What do each of them represent? Are you surrounded by free-thinkers or followers? What are the different emotions brought by your colleagues and peers? How do the conversations usually? Are they filled with positivity or with unnecessary pessimism? If you believe you are surrounded by mostly negativity, then it is time to break free of this toxic energy you have voluntarily surrounded yourself. If someone doesn't add to your growth as a person, make peace with it, talk to them, and move on. You cannot grow when others around you hold you back. Instead, surround yourself with people who bring about change, groundedness, and a sense of purpose. Seek out those with ambition and want more for their life and others.

Dealing with Adversity

Whenever faced with a challenge, it can be easy to give up or blame others for what you might lack. If you want to be a successful salesperson, then it is better you start questioning yourself. Whenever you face a setback in life, try to analyze the situation and yourself. Every setback is a lesson life is trying to teach you. Unless you learn this lesson, you are bound to make the same mistakes again. Whenever you face adversity, ask yourself, "What is good in this challenge? Then, ask yourself, "What is the lesson I have to learn?" Character growth and development occur only when you manage to learn from your mistakes. Keep in mind that adversities are unavoidable in life whereas optimism is a choice. Whenever you are faced with adversity, learn to change your response.

Try to look for some humor in every situation. Dealing with a stressful situation increases the production of cortisol (stress-inducing hormone). The best way to diffuse such tension is by looking for some humor. When you learn to deal with a stressful situation using humor, it helps put all your challenges into a proper perspective.

Taking Control

If you find yourself thinking thoughts like: "I don't have a good enough marketing strategy," "My competition is better," or "My audience is lousy," or "My territory is no good," it merely reflects your inability to solve. If you believe that something external always guides your decisions and course of action, you can never be in control of the situation. If you want to be a successful salesperson, you need to understand that you are in control of your fate. Yes, there will be some times when it's beyond your reach, but these situations will only get the better as you try to improve in your work. If business seems slow, it could be time to change your approach or redefine your efforts. Try meeting with seasoned professionals who can act like mentors in your field that are willing to share their experiences and guide you to a new approach. Stay open to change and be prepared to put in the hard work. Keep learning and improve your skills to outsell your competition. Unless you take control of your mindset, you won't get ahead in this business.

Replace the negative thoughts with more positive ones like, "I can always learn and improve my marketing strategies," "If I work hard, I can improve myself," or "I can find a way to connect with my audience." A successful salesperson knows how to manage results and take control of the situation without making excuses.

Manager Dealing with Staff

As a manager, you must be able to not just convince your subordinates to stick with your plan of action but must be able to encourage and motivate them too. If you cannot do this, then you cannot be a successful manager. Any negative thought patterns you have could effectively hold you back and prevent you from successfully managing your team. Your success as a manager depends to a great extent on your ability to make the most of your team members. Even if you give your 100% but cannot make your subordinates contribute, then it is not going to get you anywhere.

If you think others will not listen to you or don't believe in your ideas, then it shows poorly on your managerial abilities. Taking a stand for yourself and voicing your opinions with confidence makes all the difference when it comes to leadership. If you don't have confidence in your leadership abilities, then you cannot lead anyone. If you think no one will listen to you, then it will become incredibly difficult to make others listen to you.

Exercises

Challenge your Thoughts

Negativity can creep in unannounced, and it can hit you like a ton of bricks. If your thoughts often start with words like "shouldn't," "will not," or "cannot," change the conversation. Whenever you start thinking this way, challenge the reasoning behind it.

Ask yourself whether your thoughts are relevant to this moment. Is this productive?

Once you have your answer, try to replace them with a positive vision. It might take a while, but eventually, you will be able to ignore negativity and instead concentrate on working towards a positive outcome.

Conscious Monitoring

Keep in mind that you are the manager and your team members count on you for guidance and support. Therefore, it is quintessential that you consciously monitor everything you say. You don't always need to have an opinion or vocalize your thoughts. And at times, the best thing you can do is hold your tongue. For example, if you are worried about a project, then maybe it is better to express these worries later. If you start looking worried, even your team will get worried. Negativity is as contagious as positivity. So, if you can keep your emotions and words in check, it will become easier to motivate and influence your team to work in the right direction. Always learn to save your complaints about only those times when it is absolutely necessary to share them. By doing this, the chances of others rolling their eyes and ignoring you will certainly decrease. If you keep complaining all the time, then the complaint loses its power. Before you start expressing any negative thoughts, take a moment, and think about the kind of effect it would have on your team. Maybe you feel that once you express a negative thought, it will go away quickly. However, that thought can end up staying in someone else's mind for a while longer.

Breaking Down Problems

When faced with a problem, it is easy to allow your thinking to spiral out of control. If you do, it's unlikely that you will be able to control your reactions, and you will start concentrating on the things you cannot do right now. There are some things you can start working on now. Instead of worrying about what you can't do, shift your view on what you can do. Keep in mind that success brings more success. So, give yourself and your team a chance to succeed. Whenever you face a complicated problem, start breaking it down into manageable chunks. For instance, if you have a major presentation due, and there is no time to complete it, concentrate on simplifying the task at hand. Instead of one big challenge, break it down into five manageable challenges. Whenever you complete one challenge, it will give you the positivity required to face the next challenge.

So, within no time, you have completed all the tasks and successfully tackle the big challenge. This kind of thinking is not just good for you, but your team too.

An Employee Dealing With a Negative Boss

Dealing with bosses is never easy, and it is even more difficult if you deal with a difficult boss. If you want to excel in your chosen profession, learning to deal with any type of higher up is a very important skill. You might desire to be the star employee or get a job that enables you to make the most of your skillset. It is never easy working under someone unless you have a good rapport with the right person. You probably aspire to be more successful or do some meaningful work that will make others take notice of you. If you want to stand apart from the crowd, you must be able to hold your ground. Dealing with negative thoughts and paradigms can be tiring. If you have convinced yourself that your boss doesn't like you, then you might lose interest in going to work or completing work on time. If you are riddled with self-doubt and regularly question every move you make or think you aren't suited for your job and responsibilities, you are self-sabotaging.

Exercises

Feed Your Mind

Be extremely cautious of what you feed your mind and soul. Fill yourself with positivity and allow this positivity to propel you towards a positive future. If you are dealing with a negative work space or dealing with negative paradigms, find a way to change the conversation. There are different ways to do this. You can use positive affirmations or even practice simple meditation. Whenever you feel negativity creeping in, take a break from your work, and concentrate on what you need at that moment to make yourself feel better. Before you accept a thought, question it. Don't blindly accept everything that you think to be the truth.

Limit Interactions

Negativity can spread very quickly if you are not careful. To prevent this, limit your personal exchanges with the negative boss as much as you can. Don't allow them to get into your mind. If someone is affecting you, regardless of their position or yours, you have already given them permission to do so. No one can make you feel bad unless you let them. You do this, unknowingly. Therefore, make a conscious effort to keep this negative person from entering your thought patterns. Ensure that your relationship is strictly professional and don't allow your personal life to interfere. Never make things personal, and don't try to get in with someone who doesn't support you or is trustworthy. Don't try to change the way they think, and it is likely their own issues and nothing to do with you. The best you can do is try to brighten the mood when you do speak. If they try to go down the negative path, find a part in the conversation you can spin in a positive light. If it is a personal attack on you or your character, learn to stand your ground and make it known to a colleague that can help you or HR. And in the meantime become the guardian of the thoughts and energy you let into your life.

Learn to be Realistic

It is easy to assume that the people who criticize you are envious or disturbed in a completely different aspect of their own lives. Keep an open mind and try to find the base for what you are being told as there might be an underlying truth that you missed.

Even if your boss is a very critical person, their views might offer honest criticism you can learn from. Carefully reflect on the ideas you share in the workplace, and before you give someone a chance to be a critic, learn to be a critic yourself. If you're dealing with a difficult boss that looks for reasons why your ideas need work, understand being in a leadership position puts you under a magnifying glass and they are trying to get the best version of you out there. Don't feel bad about this, and don't allow the criticism to get the best of you. Instead, try to come up with constructive solutions. Think of a situation where your boss can/will point out five flaws and make sure you already have five solutions you can immediately offer.

Loner

It's never pleasant to feel like a social outcast. Maybe it makes you uncomfortable to socialize with strangers or anyone at all, and in turn, others feel uncomfortable around you. So, you might think it's easier to be alone. When you do get a chance to socialize with others, it becomes incredibly difficult for you to start a conversation or make worthwhile connections. If you feel others don't like you or that you aren't interesting enough to hold a conversation, it will harm your self-confidence, self-worth, and self-esteem.

The only problem here is your lack of skills to express yourself clearly, or an inability to love yourself. The way you present yourself is the way others will perceive you. If you come across as being weak, others will think you are. If you have zero self-confidence, then they might try to take advantage or believe they can walk all over you.

Exercises

Practice Acceptance

Learn to accept yourself the way you are. Keep in mind that you don't have to change because of what others think or believe. Everyone is entitled to their opinion and so are you. You don't have to fit into any preconceived notions others have about you or any societal notions. If something doesn't seem right to you, you can let it go. Unless you accept yourself the way you are, you cannot be happy with yourself. You cannot make friends unless you feel better about yourself. You cannot stand up for yourself and stop others from walking all over you unless you value yourself. Practice important conversations at home in the mirror or with a trusted friend to build up confidence. Everything is interconnected. So, start by accepting and loving yourself the way you are. Some people need a while longer to recharge their batteries after spending time in public. If this is applicable to you, don't worry and take the time you need. Don't feel pressured to do anything you don't want. Instead, learn to understand your likes and dislikes. Once you do this, it becomes easier to accept yourself.

Practice Self-Care

Regardless of what you do, make sure to spend some time taking care of yourself. Schedule at least 20 to 30 minutes of downtime for a self-care routine each day. By doing this, you'll notice your mood to change. Understand it's your responsibility to engage in activities you enjoy. Think of it as a detox from the external world. Keep your phone off and out of sight and concentrate on the task in front of you. Until you are comfortable with yourself, you cannot expect others to be comfortable.

Learn Quality vs. Quantity

Don't try to measure your friend circle on quantity; instead, concentrate on developing and maintaining quality relationships. Even if you just have two really good friends, it's better than being surrounded by ten people who don't care about you. So, start spending more time with the people you love. Identify any toxic relationships in your life and weed them. One meaningful conversation can make the difference in how a day plays out. It's better to be on your own than with people who constantly bring you down or drain you of your energy.

Enjoy Your Activities

Think about your early life and what you enjoyed doing before the world started getting hard. Make a list of these activities. There could be a variety of reasons why you gave up on these hobbies but there is no time like the present. Brainstorm your interests now and find new ways to learn, and make time to learn.

Maybe you always wanted to learn how to draw, paint, or play an instrument. Enroll in a class, join a club, or watch videos online. Step out of your comfort zone and interact with others. In a class setting, you will likely find someone who shares the same interests as you and you can continue to develop outside of this space. Practice interacting with others, and don't allow negative paradigms to hold you back. Make a point to talk to one stranger a day, even if it's a casual exchange. After sometime, you will feel more confident about yourself, and have the courage to interact more openly.

Entrepreneur

As an entrepreneur, your primary goal would be to establish a successful business venture. Regardless of the type of business you start, success will always be the priority, and a brilliant idea goes to waste unless you can find a way to make it real.

How do you deal with obstacles? If you are a businessperson, there will invariably be blockades on the road to success. Dealing with obstacles is an important part of life. If you cannot overcome them, keep your head up and get back in the game, you won't move ahead. If you struggle with this, then it is time to change your mindset. Your mindset influences the way you think about your life and your career. Perhaps there was a situation when you thought you had a brilliant idea, but others disagreed. In such a circumstance, viewing it as the end of the road makes you unable to move ahead. Instead, if you analyze the criticism you receive, you have a chance for improvement. Whenever you face a mistake, instead of doubting yourself, try to fix the situation at hand. Unless you change your mindset about how you view your life, success will not come your way.

Exercises

Repeat Positive Affirmations

Start your day with a few positive affirmations. Make it a point that you spend at least 5 to 10 minutes in the morning, concentrating on these. Start making a list of all the things you wish to attain and state them clearly with intention. For instance, if you want to be more successful, then concentrate on the success you want and say it out loud a couple of times daily.

Some of the affirmations you can use are:

I am successful and confident.

I might not be able to do this right now, but I will eventually get the hang of it.

This is just an obstacle, and it too shall pass like everything else in life.

I have good ideas and I can express them efficiently.

Focus on the Moment

It is easy to get overwhelmed when thinking about the past, or worrying about the future. Instead, bring yourself back to the moment. A simple exercise you can follow is to concentrate on your breathing. Whenever you feel a little overwhelmed, take a break for five minutes and concentrate on your breathing. Don't worry about your thoughts and merely allow them to pass through your mind without any judgement. It helps calm your mind. As an entrepreneur, these worries are normal, and you should expect them. Therefore, it is quintessential that you learn to deal with them. If you cannot live in the moment, then you won't see opportunities that present themselves.

Deal with Failures

The road to success is riddled with obstacles, setbacks, and different types of failures. Unless you learn to take everything in stride, you cannot expect to move ahead. The way you deal with success is as important as the way you deal with failure. Every entrepreneur dreams of success, and you must put as much preparation into failing.

If you take a moment and look at success stories of those in the spotlight, you will realize they had to overcome certain failures to get where they are. Take motivation from them and change your attitude about the way you perceive failure. Failure doesn't mean the end of the road, it is only if you choose to give up. Take it as a loss, accept it and find a way to learn from it as you rebuild. Maybe it was not meant to be for a reason.

Romantic Relationship

A relationship takes hard work. Love is important in a romantic relationship, but love can only get you so far. Beneath it is commitment, effort, patience, and the time to build a lasting relationship. If you struggle to love and accept yourself unconditionally, it will become incredibly difficult for others to love and accept you. It all starts with self-love. If you think you aren't lovable or feel others will not love you the way you are, the relationship will quickly unravel. Likewise, if you have any limiting beliefs, struggle to understand yourself, or fail to accept yourself the way you are, it will prevent you from forming lasting relationships. So, before jumping headfirst into a romantic relationship, ensure you love and accept yourself unconditionally. Any negative attitude you have towards yourself will stand in your way. It will sabotage any chance you have at success in love.

Exercises

Deal with Differences

Dealing with differences is an important part of any relationship. There will be times when you and your partner can't seem to agree or one of you is missing the point. Working through your differences and finding a way to stay together is a sign of a healthy relationship. If you are unhappy with something, then try to work on it. Ensure that the lines of communication between you and your partner are always open, honest with full transparency.

Open Up About Your Past

Take time and remember what got you to this moment. You are with your partner for a reason although sometimes it can seem easy to get bogged down by little issues, and you forget to see the good in your partner. In such a situation, you can either focus on what you believe they are doing wrong or think about the good things your partner brings to the table. No one is perfect, and expecting perfection from someone else is a recipe for disaster. So, when negativity creeps in, instead think of a good day you've shared or a moment where you felt appreciated by them. With that being said, it is never good to hold onto a toxic relationship. If all you can think about your partner are things that trouble and bother you, maybe it is time to express your doubts or fears and possibly rethink the relationship.

Express Mutual Gratitude

A relationship cannot survive if there is no respect and gratitude and it must be from both sides. Learn to be grateful for the good things your partner brings to your life. It is a great way to shift the focus of your relationship instead of allowing the negative memories linger. You can always find a way to work through fights or arguments if you want to make positive progress. In this process, don't forget to be grateful for the good times. Whenever you notice any negative thoughts about your relationship or your partner, take a break for ten minutes. Grab a paper, and start listing all the positive traits your partner possesses. Start maintaining a journal where you can write all your thoughts and feelings. Don't judge your thoughts and merely allow them to flow. It helps clear your mind and regain some perspective. Don't forget to write the good and bad about your relationship and partner. The next time you feel overwhelmed, merely go through these points and you will feel better.

Group Leader

Groups exist in many different settings and scenarios. We all like being around those with whom we share certain similarities. Being a group leader in a social setting means you are the one in control. Just like a manager in a professional setting, you will be the decision-maker and the risk-taker in a social setting too. Unless you are comfortable in this role, you cannot be a good leader. If you cannot make others listen to your suggestions or convince them to follow your ideas, you cannot be a good leader. This can feel like a lot of pressure. It is not just about meeting others expectations, but also providing solutions and good advice to those who look to you for help.

Harboring any negative thoughts about your abilities and skills will certainly become an obstacle in such a situation. If you think your ideas are worthless or they aren't worth sharing with others, you will quickly go from being a leader to a loner. If you aren't comfortable with yourself, then you cannot make others comfortable around you. Any negative thoughts and the negative self-talk you indulge in will damage your self-confidence.

Exercises

Communicate Efficiently

Communication is key in this scenario. Perhaps it is one of the major influences you can exert on those around you. As a leader, you influence more than you realize and your words go a long way. If you regularly encourage and congratulate others, it sets a positive tone for your position and how you help your team succeed.

Empower Others

To be a good group leader, you must work on empowering others. It is not just your development that matters, but the development of those around you. Share your knowledge, try to help others improve, and you will feel better about yourself. By doing this, it creates an environment of positivity and growth.

Take Responsibility

Accepting responsibility is an important part of being a leader. It is not just applicable for success but failures as well. If you make a mistake, own up and make amends. Ensure that you don't make the same mistake again. Until you can take responsibility for your mistakes, you cannot grow as a person. It is quite easy to blame others when things go south or take credit for good outcomes. However, a good leader knows that accepting responsibility and knowing how to share the praise with your team are important factors.

Understand Gratitude Matters

Whenever someone does a task well or goes that extra mile, find creative ways to express gratitude and reinforce good behavior. Acknowledging the hard work of others, and being thankful is a small thing that goes a long way. It could be saying thank you, smiling or awarding special privileges. It may seem insignificant but they will enhance the group's attitude towards you.

Show Some Empathy

If you want to be a successful leader, then you must be able to show some empathy. It's important to develop and maintain good relationships. Once you understand where the other person is coming from, it becomes easier to see their perspective. Just because you are empathetic, it doesn't mean you always have to agree with others. However, it does give you a better insight into what's going on and makes you more approachable as a leader.

Parent

As a parent, you are not only responsible for your child's wellbeing, but their steady growth. Since children are impressionable, the way you think, feel, and behave around them influences their behavior, thought process, and how they express emotion. Unless you set the right example for your child early on, you cannot expect them to become a proper member of society alone. Leading by example is the only way to ensure their future is bright.

There will be times when your children just don't want to listen to you. These little incidents can add up making you doubt your skills as a parent. And naturally when your child excels, you will feel better about your ability to get through to them. If an when your child stumbles or falls, you can't allow this negativity to harm your ideas of parenting and the skills you've honed. If you worry too much about being a good parent, you are more likely to make mistakes. Regardless of what you want to believe, children don't come with a manual and feel better knowing you will figure out more as you go.

Exercises

In this section, let us look at simple exercises you can follow to change any of your negative thought patterns.

Manage Your Expectations

Learn to manage your expectations while dealing with a child. At times, it is quite easy to forget that you are dealing with a child. You cannot expect a child to behave like an adult. Therefore, you cannot talk to your child the way you talk to an adult. If you don't manage your expectations, you will merely be setting yourself up for this appointment. Not just that, it can adversely affect the way your child feels about himself. If you set him up for impossible tasks or age-inappropriate tasks, he will fail. In that situation, it is not just your self-esteem, as a parent, but even your child's self-esteem will take a backseat. The only way to teach your child proper behavior is by modeling desirable behavior. Perhaps you expect your child to sit through a long meal and display proper table manners. However, if you expect a toddler to do this, you are merely setting yourself up for disappointment. Therefore, it is time to lower your expectations. Expect from your child only what he can deliver.

Know It's a Phase

When it comes to parenting, everything is a phase. Initially, a newborn will struggle to sleep through the night until he learns to do this. A teenager is bound to go through a rebellious phase. As a child is growing, he will ask you plenty of questions that can become slightly annoying. All these things are merely phases of growing up. Make your peace, and it becomes easier to deal with all this. If you are having a tough time getting your child to sleep through the night without waking up in the middle, then it merely means your child needs some time to learn this. Keep in mind that your child is learning as he is growing. You cannot expect him to behave like an adult. Therefore, whenever you feel like you are running into any difficulties, remind yourself. It is just a phase. As with everything in life, this too shall pass.

Rethink the Problem

If you want to maintain a positive attitude while parenting, it is always important you thoroughly understand your perception of the problem. At times, the simplest thing you can do is merely change the way you perceive a problem, and everything becomes easier. Take a moment and think about something your child does that triggers you. Perhaps it is your toddler's shrieking, or maybe you are upset that your teenager never listens to you. Try to understand what your child is getting out of such a situation. Perhaps your child is behaving in a way that you consider to be bad because he wants your attention, or he's looking for a reaction. If he is merely trying to get your attention, then he will be happy even if it is a negative reaction. If you react angrily, he will merely keep at it. Now, it is time to think about why the specific behavior seems to bother you. Perhaps you are bothered by it because it embarrasses you in front of others or because society views it as unacceptable. Let go of these preconceived notions you have in your mind. A child is bound to do all this, and as a parent, you must correct him, instead of trying to control him.

Change Your Perception

A common mistake a lot of parents make is that they try to parent the child they wish they had instead of the one they have. Forget about all the ideas you had about your child and learn to parent the one you have. Forget about everything and learn to stay in the moment. Keep in mind that every child is different, and they have certain flaws and strengths. Your style of parenting must fit your child's needs, and not any of the preconceived notions you have about parenting. Just because your child isn't able to pick up on something new right away, it doesn't reflect poorly on your parenting skills. Keep in mind that you can only guide your child to do their best. Don't equate their success with that of yourself as a parent. Keep these things separate in your mind, and parenting will get easier.

Marketer

A marketer's aim, as with a salesperson, is to increase sales. You aren't doing your job as a marketer efficiently if you cannot successfully market your products to potential customers. If you have any limiting beliefs about your skills as a marketer, others will be able to see right through it. Perhaps you doubt your ideas and abilities. Or maybe you have convinced yourself you don't have the skills required to be a good marketer. All these instances are representations of your negative beliefs. If you want to attain your goal of being a good marketer, then you must let go of such thought patterns.

Exercises

Learn from Mistakes

There will be times when things don't work out the way you want them to. You will make mistakes, and even the best marketing plans can fail. In such moments, the only thing that matters is the way you deal with the mistake. You can either learn from the mistake and move on or continue to dwell and feel worse Don't allow a mistake or a setback to prevent you from accomplishing your goals. For instance, if you worked hard on a marketing campaign, but it didn't produce the results you wished, then it is time for some contemplation. Think of it as a setback and not a failure. Grab a sheet of paper and divide it into four columns. In the first column, write the action you took, the second column includes information about the desired outcome, the third column is about the desired outcome, and the fourth column is about all the things you wish you would have done differently.

Reflect

Before you start working on anything new, take a couple of minutes to visualize the outcome you want to achieve with this task. There must always be some form of scope for reflection. Unless you are aware of your performance, and analyze the outcome you cannot improve. So, when plans change as you start working, look back at your goals and understand the action you must now take to keep moving ahead. You will avoid taking on more tasks than you can handle and increase productivity. Having a plan in mind, you can complete things in a specific order one at a time, moving onto another in a timely manner. Multitasking is not the key to success for everyone as with some people it reduces your overall productivity. For instance, if you have to complete ten tasks within the next two days, start by making a list of all these tasks. Then start scoring these tasks according to their importance (one being most important and ten being the least important). By doing this, you can start prioritizing the tasks. Don't forget to cross items off this list whenever you complete one task. By doing this, you can successfully accomplish more within a given timeframe.

Be Open to Change

As a marketer, you must be open to change. You cannot get stuck in your ideals or notions of how things are supposed to be. Instead, make it a point to learn and adapt to a situation. If you want to be successful, be a sponge, learn, and change. It is important to continue transforming in order to stay relevant. You cannot be at the top of the game by merely reusing the same techniques and tactics. Therefore, be ready to adapt to the latest trends and track new strategies to improve your overall game. For instance, the world of marketing has certainly revolutionized since the introduction of the internet. These days, marketing is not just restricted to conventional print media and offline marketing. You must focus on online marketing too. By understanding the different platforms your target audience frequents, you can effectively develop a marketing strategy suitable for the concerned platform. Unless you are open to change, you cannot do this.

Student

There might be times in life when you feel prepared for an exam or class and even after studying and applying new learning techniques your grades don't reflect your effort. Maybe you compare yourself to the other students and feel discouraged when you see they are doing better. Perhaps you feel like you are letting yourself down. Any negative belief like "I am not smart enough to crack this test," or "I will fail even if I study," will effectively hold you back from even making an effort.

Instead of thinking these negative thoughts, replace them with positive statements like, "If I study hard, I can do better," "I have come a long way since I started," or "Even if I don't do well now, I can always improve myself."

As a student in a university your goal is to excel in your chosen major but we all play the role of a student throughout our lives. It is not just in school and college when we are forced to learn.

If you want to get ahead in life, you cannot stop learning and finding new ways to let go of such negative thought patterns.

Exercises

Take a Minute

Maintaining a positive and peaceful environment is important. It is quite easy to complain about any tests or work you must complete. During such situations, emotions can run high, and you can feel overwhelmed. Try to stay calm and don't jump to conclusions before you start on a specific assignment or a project. If you're already thinking negatively, take a break from the situation and try to refocus your reactions.

Take Pride

It is quite easy to allow negative thinking to bring you down. Once negative thinking gets a hold of you, it becomes difficult to see any positivity. To rewire any negative thinking, it is important to build a positive approach towards what you are trying to learn. The best way to do this is by complimenting yourself on your achievements and concentrating on what's coming next. If you are too hard on yourself because you failed a test, take the necessary actions to do better on the next one to boost your grade or see if extra assignments are available as credit. When you complete an assignment on time, congratulate yourself even if you don't do as well as you hoped. Maintain a positive attitude towards honing your skills, and all the effort you make, and it will reflect in your improved self-esteem. Once you feel better about yourself, the effort you make will automatically improve.

Think Positive

Any effort you make is directly associated with your attitude. If you want to change any of your negative paradigms in life, then it is time you concentrate on positive aspects.

Think about the lessons you learned from a negative situation in life.

Rewire your mind and inculcate the habit of positive thinking, it is time to change your internal voice.

When you find your mind is playing against your natural born ability to succeed, try out some of these practices to do that:

- If you think you cannot do something, remind yourself to at least try. If you feel like you don't fully grasp a new topic ask your teacher after class to explain it to you again or look into tutoring. Even if it takes you longer than your peers to learn, it doesn't reflect on your intelligence level.
- If you don't like a specific subject change your line of thinking into something like: "This subject is difficult for me, but once I have all the available materials, I can start to improve."
- There will be times when you can't get everything done, change your thoughts to: "The more homework I complete, the more will I learn about a topic."
- If you think you aren't smart enough, then change the thought to: "I will keep trying, and practicing until I become successful."

Politician

Regardless of whether you are a seasoned politician running for a senate seat or running for student council, you must have the qualities of a good leader. The primary aim of any politician would be to effectively hold onto their existing supporters while increasing their supporter base. To do this, you need to have the power to sway public opinion. Even if you have brilliant ideas, you cannot become a successful politician, unless you express them efficiently. If you are regularly plagued by limiting beliefs and don't trust your abilities, then it will quickly show up in the way you act, think, and behave. Unless you exude confidence, you cannot expect others to believe you. You need public favor, and any negative paradigms or preconceived limiting beliefs will stop you from attaining this goal.

Exercises

Differentiate Fact from Fiction

If you want to rewire your thinking and make it more positive, then it is time to understand yourself. You must learn to understand your negative thought paradigms. Learn to differentiate what is real and what is your mind running away with pieces of information. Often, most of the thoughts are based on certain assumptions we have formed about ourselves, the situation, and the world in general. Unless you identify what is true and what is just an assumption, you cannot become successful. It is quite easy to believe that others don't like your ideas or that you are not capable of leading. Well, this is nothing but an assumption you have formed about yourself. In such situations, ask yourself where your thoughts come from. Once you manage to understand these are your thoughts, but not public opinion, you will feel better about yourself. Your thoughts shape your behavior, so, it is quintessential that you understand what facts are and what is fiction.

Practice Performance and Not Politics

Instead of allowing yourself to get bogged down by all the politics and different games people play, learn to concentrate on your performance. In the end, your performance is the only thing that determines your success. Unfortunately, most politicians start believing that they must manage their politics instead of concentrating on performance.

Once you have formulated certain goals, stay on track, and try to achieve those goals. The minute you achieve a goal, it gives you the positivity to keep going. So, whenever you feel bogged down, you can remind yourself of all the good you have managed to accomplish. Regardless of what your opponents say, keep in mind is all this is politics. Don't allow it to get the better of you and, instead, learn to manage it. Start maintaining a journal to remind yourself of the progress you make. Start listing out all the different things that you managed to accomplish, regardless of how minute it might be. Once you do this, you will have a list of accomplishments you can refer to whenever your motivation starts running low.

Challenge Convention

The only way you can make an impact in this world is by challenging the conventional. There are plenty of opinions on how a politician should behave. There are ways in which society influences the way you think about yourself. Instead of allowing all these conventions to guide your journey as a politician, it is time you try challenging these conventions. Be willing to take on risks and challenge any pre-existing notions. If you strongly believe in something, and you know you are right, then stand your ground. It can be quite tempting to assume a herd mentality and follow what others are doing. Instead, remember you are the leader, and people will follow you if you believe in yourself. If you are willing to change and are attempting to bring about a positive change, then focus on the outcomes, and it will give you the motivation to keep going.

While practicing these exercises, keep in mind that it takes plenty of conscious effort, consistency, and motivation to change negative thought paradigms. So, learn to be patient with yourself and don't get frustrated. Start following the simple tips discussed in this section to attain your goals in different roles you play in life. Once you start following these simple tips, you can see a positive change in yourself and your life in general.

Rewire
Your Mind

Rewire Your Brain to Become a Manipulator. A Workbook to Discover Your Personality and Change Your Mind

Richard Empath

CHAPTER 1:

Importance of Mindset

Success vs. Failure

There exists a precise distinction between those who are successful and those who just wish for success. The primary difference lies in the habits. Habits influence every decision made by an individual, which will either be remembered or forgotten by others. By merely adjusting and tweaking your thought patterns to resemble the ones demonstrated by successful people will not only influence your life but also show how others perceive you. A successful person is willing to do all that a hopeful person often hesitates to do. There are different elements associated with success, and it isn't limited to hard work. It is so much more than just the desire to be successful. It is about having the courage to take the necessary action to make a difference. Here are some differences between those who succeed and those who don't, do any sound familiar?

Embrace Change

One of the major differences between those who are successful or unsuccessful is the way they deal with change. The only thing constant in life, and if you want to grow, you must embrace change. Change is seldom easy, but sometimes you get a break. When you have to step out of your comfort zone, it becomes tricky. Instead of denying, hiding, or fearing the unknown, try to embrace and adapt it, and your life will become easier.

Accept Responsibility

A successful person never blames others for their failure; they accept responsibility for it, whereas an unsuccessful person often looks at others or external factors to take the blame. If you want to be successful, then understand that failure is part and parcel of this process. You must accept responsibility for not just your success, but also your mistakes and failures. When you blame others, it merely brings them down, and there's no good that can come out of a situation like that.

Embrace the Team

Instead of talking about people, start talking about ideas. Idle gossip will get you nowhere; instead, start discussing your dreams, passions, even confusions. Sharing ideas with others can help you make sense of things, it will do you good and lead to another's growth as well. Successful people don't wish for others to fail; rather, they want to see and help the people in their space succeed. Just because someone else is doing well doesn't mean you are nothing. If you work in a team, then your team will not see success unless every member is putting in effort.

Celebrate Others

Successful people give others due credit for any victories, whereas unsuccessful people want all the credit. It is okay to let others have their time to shine. It will eventually lead to a better performance. A successful person tries to help others, whereas an unsuccessful one only seeks to help themselves. Instead of worrying about how others can help you, concentrate on what you can do for them. By merely offering assistance, you tend to come across as warm, helpful, and likable. This is a common trait displayed by successful people.

Keep Learning

Learning is an ongoing process, and it doesn't end when your education does. Be a sponge and soak it all in and try to learn something new every day. Never stop learning if you want to grow and get ahead in life. A successful person certainly knows the importance of learning and knowledge. The more flexible and curious you are, the easier it is to step above your competition. Instead of being reactive, be proactive and take charge today. If you sit within your comfort zone, then even when opportunities come knocking at your door, you cannot see them.

Take Risks

Fear of failure can be paralyzing, and it can prevent anyone from taking risks. You cannot expect rewards unless you take risks. It is one of the areas where successful people are different from the others. They live by the motto: if you don't try, you will never know. At times, all you have to do is take the first step to gain momentum. If you are worried about failure, you won't move forward. Instead of thinking of failure as the end of the road, know it is a chance for improvement and growth.

Be Transparent

Successful people are open and transparent. They aren't scared to be vulnerable, and it is a more appealing trait. On the other hand, unsuccessful people tend to be very secretive and seldom show their true colors. Showing emotions is not a sign of weakness. Unless you are comfortable with the feelings you have, you cannot learn to regulate them. A successful person has complete control over their emotions and isn't worried about displaying them constructively. Sincere emotions are powerful enough to trigger an emotional response. A successful person certainly knows this and isn't afraid to use emotion when necessary.

Learn Self-Awareness

Successful people always look for different ways to get a better understanding of themselves and other people seldom care about self-introspection. Before you learn to influence others to get what you desire in your life, you must understand yourself. We tend to have unconscious motivations that impact all our decisions. Unless you know yourself, you cannot attain any of your goals.

Good Listener

An underrated life skill is listening. Everyone likes to talk, but not many people are good listeners. Since we get so excited about our ideas, all we wish to do is keep talking about them. However, the less you talk, the easier it is to persuade others to accept your ideas and yourself in general. The key to building rapport with anyone is to be a good listener. Unless you are willing to listen, why would others want to listen to what you have to say?

Have a Positive Attitude

Thriving people know the importance of always maintaining a positive attitude while others are likely to default to negativity. Positivity is contagious, especially when it comes from someone in a position of power or authority. For instance, how do you react when someone asks you how you are doing? Instead of saying, "I am fine," try saying, "I am fantastic." By merely changing the way you respond to a situation, you can change the way others react to you. It is a great skill that comes in handy while influencing others to get ahead in life. Always maintain a positive attitude. If you look at a glass and notice how much it can be filled, that shows scope for improvement.

Be Kind

Successful people are often committed to acts of gratitude and compassion, whereas unsuccessful people always put themselves first. Instead of trying to get everything you want, treat others well, and you will, with time, get everything you desire. Never let go of an opportunity to be grateful. There are plenty of things in your life to be thankful for; always remind yourself the same. Never forget to thank all those people who helped you along the way to attain your goals.

Be Less Critical

People seldom stop to appreciate others and the world around them, whereas successful people embrace every aspect of their life and appreciate it's intricacy. Start looking for ways to compliment others instead of looking at their faults and being critical. It is okay to challenge and offer criticism to those who are open to it sometimes. However, it can't be the only thing you give to others. Self-criticism or criticizing others merely brings down overall spirit and morale if it's the only thing people expect of you. Instead, focus on only the good things others can offer you and speak kindly. It will not only make others feel better, but it leads to more positivity in your life.

Forgive and Forget

We are all human, and that means we are inherently good at making mistakes and they do happen often. If you dwell on these bumps in the road or errors made by others, it will only build resentment. Unless you learn to let go, you cannot move ahead in life. Holding onto petty grudges will do you no favors, it will fester an endless cycle of hurt and negativity. A successful person knows the importance of the concept to forgive and forget. Learn your lessons from your past, make peace, move on, and try not to repeat them in the future. It is not about ignoring your emotions; it is about working through them. Learn your lessons, make the changes, and don't dwell on the past.

After going through the list of differences, you might have noticed that most of the attributes associated with success are about the mindset. Mindset is the difference between those who succeed and fail. If you want to be successful in life, start tweaking your mindset today. You will learn more about rewiring your brain and changing your mindset in the subsequent chapters.

CHAPTER 2:

All About the Mind

Mind vs. Brain

Use your left index finger to point to your brain. Easy, right? Now, point to your mind using the same finger. You probably hesitated because you never realized there is a difference between the brain and the mind. While it is quite easy to pinpoint the physical location of the brain, it is rather difficult to understand where the mind exists. Understandably, all those who don't have a degree in neurobiology would use the terms brain and mind synonymously. You talk about feeling, thinking, remembering, and dreaming but when using these terms, you are not referring to your brain. When using the mind to describe something, you might say, "I recognized my babysitter in a crowd last week because she was wearing a long necklace, which is so weird that I remember it now."

You would not say, "A stream of photons appeared on my retina, triggering the optic nerve to carry an electrical signal with it to the lateral geniculate body and then the primary visual cortex. These signals were sent to my striate cortex, where the color and orientation of the image were determined. Then this signal was sent to my inferotemporal and prefrontal cortex where the object was recognized from my memories, causing me to recognize my babysitter." Now, this is an instance of brain talk. There certainly exists an interconnection between the brain and the mind. The mind is believed to be identical to one's feelings, beliefs, thoughts, memories, and behaviors. It is not made of any physical materials, but it is incredibly powerful.

The brain is made of soft tissue, weighing about 3 pounds, and is present within the skull. It is the physical source of the mind. If you have a specific thought or feel an emotion, it is because your brain has relayed an electrical signal along a string of neurons, and these neurons provide certain neurochemicals to cause the specific thought or emotion. It is almost the way a runner in a relay race hands over the baton to the next runner.

A computer needs hardware to work, and hardware requires software to function. The hardware will be rendered useless without the software, and the software cannot work without the hardware, etc. So, in this scenario the mind is the software and the brain the hardware. However, the difference between these two concepts is more complicated than that comparison and these terms have overlapping meanings. As mentioned previously, the brain is an organ and physical residence of the mind. It helps with coordinating movements, transmitting signals, and takes care of the upkeep of the physical body. We use our mind to think about the past, present, and future.

You might have come across stories about the unbelievable powers of the mind, from miraculous remissions of chronic illnesses via mind and body interactions to Herculean feats of strength during a moment of panic and showing incredible perseverance during hardships. It is also responsible for significant insights and epiphanies that seem to appear out of the blue with new creative and inventive ideas. Therefore, it is not surprising that in quiet moments, we often think about the meaning of life and our place in the universe. Any thoughts about how wonderful certain food tastes to how beautiful nature looks are questions that often lead to a deeper one - what is the mind and what power does it have? Philosophers and great thinkers throughout history, as well as scientists in the modern era, have been trying to answer these questions. It is an orthodox belief in the scientific community that the mind or consciousness is a byproduct of all the electrochemical activity taking place in the brain. Now, this is just a belief and hasn't been proven yet but there is plenty of debate in the scientific community. Rupert Sheldrake, a visionary biologist, thought that the mind being present in the brain is a principle that people accepted without question. Sir Julian Huxley, a popular biologist during the 1900s, was asked whether the brain was a good way to describe the mind. He answered that the brain is not the only thing responsible for the mind. Even though it is the precursor for its manifestation, he believed that when the brain is isolated, it is merely a biological organ that is rendered meaningless the way an isolated individual is.

There is no doubt the brain is important for the proper functioning of certain aspects of the mind. For instance, any damage to the brain, injury, or illness, can affect one's ability to remember, reason, think logically, and so on. However, there are frontier scientists who believe the mind is not entirely dependent on the brain for its existence. The mind seems to exist beyond the brain, and even outside the physical body. After all, the concept of collective and global conscience does exist. Frontier science believes the mind must be considered to be a form of energy and information that is not only spread through every single cell in the human body but beyond the body and connects to the entire universe and everything present within.

So, this belief tells us the brain and, through extension, the mind is not just restricted to the skull. These days, the paradigms of biology are slowly changing, especially about the different chemicals released by the brain. Depending upon the way you think and feel, the brain produces certain biochemicals. These biochemicals are known as neuropeptides and often dubbed as molecules of emotion. They're essentially messenger molecules, and how your thoughts transform themselves into these molecules affect your entire body.

For instance, whenever you feel anxious, your body produces its own type of Valium to calm you down. When you feel exhilarated, it produces a molecule known as interleukin-2. The levels of interleukin-2 reduce whenever you feel stressed. Why does all this matter? Well, interleukin-2 is an immune system booster and is believed to have certain anti-cancer properties. Stress tends to reduce the levels of this helpful chemical and thereby compromises your immune system. It certainly is a good reason to maintain a more positive attitude in your life and take less stress.

At least on the molecular level, your mood directly affects your immune system. Every thought or emotion has a biochemical counterpart to it. So, your body has different chemicals designed for anger, love, happiness, lust, guilt, and so on. At one point, it was believed that these molecules of emotion were manufactured only by the nervous system and the brain. However, ongoing research in this field shows other systems in the body influence every cell present within and not just the nervous system.

So, it is safe to say that the mind, in a literal sense, describes an overall body phenomenon. One can also conclude that the physical body is merely an extension of the subconscious mind. Instead of thinking of the brain as the commander and chief of the body, our emotions, perceptions, and thoughts guide the brain to produce the required molecules. Therefore, the mind works through the brain to organize and coordinate different metabolic functions required for survival. If you think of the brain as the guitar, then the mind is the guitarist playing the music reverberating throughout your body.

The Conscious and the Unconscious Mind

Low self-worth, restricting beliefs, perfectionism, procrastination, or failing to achieve are issues associated with the mindset. As mentioned in the previous chapter, the only difference between success and failure is how you perceive it. However, before you can learn how to do this, it helps to get a better understanding of what is going on within your head.

Let us move a little further with the hardware and software analogy. If you have a computer in your head, then the brain is the housing, whereas your mind controls this hardware. Your brain has all the wiring, processing power, connections, memory, and storage you require to function. Whereas your mind is the operating system that helps gather, store, and manage all the data using the processing resources present in the brain. The brain and the mind are two integral aspects of the same entity, and you cannot effectively operate without either of them. The human brain contains billions of neurons, which creates the central nervous system. All these nerve cells help transmit and receive electrochemical signals that essentially form your actions, thoughts, emotions, and other automatic functions of your body. To put things in perspective, 100 billion sand grains can fill 5,000,000 teaspoons and weigh about two metric tons. Even though it is packed with over 100 billion neurons, the brain is roughly the size of a cauliflower. The thoughts produced by your mind depend on your brain software. It is believed that there are different levels of consciousness in your mind, and they are the conscious mind and the unconscious mind.

The Conscious Mind

The conscious mind accounts for less than 10 percent of the total operational power of your mind. It is responsible for the following functions:

- Gathering information
- Assessing and processing the data you collect
- Creating and noticing patterns while making comparisons
- Decision-making skills
- Enabling thoughtful responses to situations instead of reactions
- Regulating short-term memory

Whenever something is present in your conscious mind, it is often deliberate, and you are always aware of it.

The Unconscious Mind

The other 90% of software your brain requires to function is your unconscious mind. It might feel a little inaccessible since you're not consciously aware of whatever goes on in there, but it is incredibly powerful. Most of the body functions are controlled by the unconscious mind like digestion, breathing, heart rate, temperature, sleeping, blinking, and so on. All these functions carry on regardless of whether you are aware of it consciously or not. You don't have to lift a finger to start any of these functions, and they go on until your last breath. The unconscious mind tries to maintain the status quo, and it is the reason why you feel uncomfortable while dealing with change. Your mind tries to steer you back to all that it is familiar with, and safe. Your unconscious mind is the center of all your emotions, creativity, and imagination.

All the habits you create and maintain are also a resultant action of this unconscious mind. However, the subconscious can be influenced by any commands given by the conscious mind. The unconscious mind also helps to store and retrieve any long-term memories. Unlike the conscious mind, which is the seat of rationalism, the unconscious is seldom rational. Your decisions and judgments don't stem from here, it merely accepts what it is told as the truth, regardless of the credibility. Once your mind accepts something to be true, all your thoughts, emotions, and behaviors will be consistent with that truth.

So, why should you feel the need to understand how the mind works? Because knowledge is power. The more knowledge you have, the more control you will have over your conscious and unconscious mind. When you understand how it works, will you be able to change yourself and affect another person's train of thought. Only by learning to combine and harness the true potential of your conscious and unconscious mind, you can make things happen.

The mind is merely the manifestation of your perceptions, thoughts, memories, imagination, and determination. All of this takes place within its physical housing unit - the brain.

Your mind has an awareness of consciousness that you know, the ability to control what you do and know your reasons for doing the same. It gives you the ability to understand. Animals can interpret their environment but cannot understand it.

On the other hand, humans can understand whatever happens around them and adapt accordingly. The mind enables us to solve complicated problems using the logic that sets us apart from other living beings. Logic gives us the power to understand things as they are instead of what is seen. Our innate ability to analyze situations helps us develop solutions and practical plans to steer clear of any problems.

We might not be able to see the ultraviolet light but can design instruments that help us do so. We cannot see atoms but can design experiments that enable us to understand their properties. With every stage of scientific advancement, humans have tried to come to a logical conclusion consistent with all their observations. Gone are the days when we believed evils and demons to be the cause of illnesses. We now know, bacteria, genetic defects, and environmental factors and viruses all play a role in ailments and disease. All this is possible because of a combination between the rational brain and the unconscious mind.

CHAPTER 3:

Thoughts and Actions

Link Between Thoughts, Decisions, Actions, and Results

There exists a strong link between your thoughts, decisions, actions, and reality. They form a never-ending cycle of reactions as your ideas influence your decision-making skills. Your choices shape the actions you take, and actions impact reality influencing thought patterns. So, it is safe to say that your thoughts also influence your reality. You will learn more about this interdependent relationship here.

There might have been times in your life where you look at a situation and wonder how you got there. At times, it could be something as simple as eating ice cream when you promised yourself you wouldn't. Other times, it could be a major decision with significant consequences like impulsively quitting your job with no safety net. To understand how your thoughts truly affect your life, you need to understand their connection.

Thoughts

All the information around you is absorbed by the brain, which is then processed to form your thoughts. Your mind is essentially the gatekeeper of all the information present around you. It decides the relevance of this information and thereby decides which thoughts must get your mental focus. Thoughts can easily transform themselves into beliefs that influence our feelings. This influence can be negative, j as well as positive. Let us take the example of bingeing on ice cream. Perhaps the thought was simply, "I had a rough day, and I deserve something nice," or "I'm starving and this is my quickest option right now."

Feelings

Any emotional response to your thoughts or behaviors is known as a feeling. These act as indicators of your connection to a given situation. Feelings originate from past experiences as well as current perspective. Things start getting a little tricky when you take a simple thought, "I am hungry," and add an emotional response to that thought. A lot of times we end up combining emotions from several other factors onto one specific thought, which really has nothing to do with that emotion. Thinking "I'm hungry," can have other connotations if linked to grief after receiving some bad news, stress from a hectic day, or anger from a fight.

Behaviors

The actions resulting from thoughts and feelings are known as behaviors. The way you behave is important because your thoughts are telling you that it is the best option at a given point. So, if you feel hungry, and feel stressed or sad, you might decide eating ice cream is the best way to deal with your emotions.

These three different aspects are interconnected, and one cannot exist without the other. So, when you start thinking about the impact your thoughts have, you will realize how much they affect your entire life. Thoughts not only trigger emotions but also guide your behavioral responses. Your perception of yourself and the world are altered by the way you feel. It, in turn, affects the way you respond to a given situation.

Your emotions and feelings guide your behavior, and your thoughts and beliefs guide your responses. You cannot act unless you have an idea on which you wish to initiate action and context as well. There's always a reason why we do the things that we do. Actions are never baseless, even if they seem completely random they are always caused by something even if you aren't aware of what. This something essentially relates to your feelings, emotions, thoughts, and beliefs. So, if you suddenly experience sadness, you might react in a specific way. If you feel angry or sad, your response will usually stem from your feelings at that moment. If you believe that someone should or should not do something, then your behavior might be triggered by your beliefs. For instance, if someone accidentally bumps into you, and you think they owe you an apology, and when they don't, your reaction if any will be triggered by your beliefs.

At times, you might be aware of any feelings or beliefs you have, and at times they are the result of underlying feelings you haven't processed yet. Feelings and beliefs don't appear out of thin air and have specific causes. They are generated from experience and starts from the moment you take your first breath until your last. Things will continue to happen, and we continue to come up with ideas about ourselves as well as the world around us. These experiences influence the way we feel about ourselves and the world.

For instance, a young child might be playing in the backyard, and after some time, decides to climb up a tree without success. Then, one day, he manages to scramble up the tree. He feels exuberant and triumphant in his success. He thinks it's the best time, he is having fun and feels safe. Then, suddenly, one of his parents comes out of the house and shouts at him for being in the tree. They tell him it's dangerous and he must never climb the tree again or will end up hurting himself. What is the child thinking at this moment? He is young, unsure, and doesn't fully understand the world around him so it could be any of the following:

- Having fun or feelings of fun are not safe.
- The world outside is dangerous.
- My parents don't want me to have fun.
- They are unhappy when I am having fun.
- I am not necessarily safe, even when I think I am.
- I will hurt myself if I have fun.
- It is dangerous to do things alone.
- It is not a good idea to try anything new.
- My parents don't think I can do anything.

As time passes, the child might forget the decisions he made or the belief that was formed because of it. Although he won't always recall that memory it will be lodged in his subconscious in some way. Any other event or experience that reinforces this belief will slowly form his attitude towards life. So, there might be a time when the child is having fun with his friends and starts feeling uncomfortable about a good situation he is in. He starts to withdraw, and the previous beliefs he has formed about fun is preventing him from having it now. He might not even remember why he feels this way, but he knows he doesn't like it. As he grows up, he might think that he's not supposed to trust himself or the decisions he makes. And all this is because of a simple misunderstanding. This example, as mentioned earlier, is an instance of how beliefs are formed and the way they influence decision-making, actions, and results.

Once you understand the relationship between your thought process and actions, you give yourself a chance to choose your reactions. It, in turn, allows you to change because you know you have a choice. You can work on understanding your feelings, become more conscious about your decisions, and take action. There are three important things you must keep in mind while understanding this relationship.

The first thing you must do is validate your feelings. Regardless of what it is, never ignore the way things make you feel. If you wish to change something about yourself, the first step is to acknowledge and accept. If you feel sad or depressed, don't allow anyone to tell you otherwise. It is okay to feel sad or depressed. As soon as you accept your feelings, it becomes easier to work on changing them. When you understand what you feel and why you feel, you can take corrective action.

The second step is to guide your thinking. There's one thing you can always control, and that is the way you think. Your brain merely absorbs information, but it is a conscious decision to form thoughts. You can control your thoughts, and it must never be the other way around. If you allow your thoughts to control you, your life will become chaotic.

The third step is action. You cannot hold yourself accountable for the way you feel or the way you think. However, you can and will always be held responsible for the way you act. Your behavior, performance, actions, and the results are all dependent on you. If you get angry at someone and lash out physically, you will be held accountable for any altercation. Once you understand what it means to be accountable, it becomes easier to make corrective action. By merely changing the way you look at a problem, you can come up with a wide range of solutions.

CHAPTER 4:

Paradigm is Important

What Is a Paradigm?

A paradigm is almost like a program or software installed in your subconscious mind. It is responsible for controlling your habits and behaviors, apart from your thinking patterns. If you take a moment and think about it, almost all your behavior is based on habit. From the moment you wake up in the morning until you go to sleep at night, you follow a specific routine. You might make breakfast, drink coffee, scroll on social media or read the news, work, exercise, eat, relax, and sleep then do it all again the next day. These are considered your habits. The different aspects of life your paradigms influence include your sense of perception, overall effectiveness, use of time, productivity, logical thinking, and creativity. A paradigm essentially places each of these areas in a box, and regardless of how hard you try, you cannot break these boxes until you change your mental programming.

We all have different paradigms, but seldom do we create them ourselves. We either inherit them, or they are dependent on environmental conditioning. Your mental programming trickles down to you from the DNA of your parents and their ancestors, going back for generations together. Every single thing you are exposed to becomes a part of your paradigms. As you go through life, everything that happens is programmed into your mind. Any ideas you are presented in your life becomes a part of your paradigms as they are like seeds that get planted into the soil of your subconscious.

How to Change Your Paradigm?

There are some things you need to understand about your paradigms. The first that we mentioned is they are the result of several habits and if you wish to change it, then you must change it the way it was created, by repetition. This desire to change your paradigms must be deliberate and conscious. You must strive to replace an undesirable habit with a positive one. Habits are neither formed nor exist in a vacuum, so there are different things to take into consideration.

To change your standards, start a conscious process of selecting a new belief aligned with the habits you wish to learn and replace the previous views. A simple way to do this is by using affirmations. These are positive statements that reflect your behaviors or new beliefs you want to incorporate into your life. An affirmation is repeated several times until it becomes embedded in your subconscious. Another simple tool you can use to change your paradigms is visualization. If you are trying to create a new self-image, then visualize how you will feel once you have attained this goal. Start picturing the kind of life you want to lead and start living your life in that manner. Visualization gives your subconscious mind a goal to strive towards. Once the message is embedded in your subconscious, then every action you take either knowingly or unknowingly will be guided by that goal. Here is another simple exercise you can follow:

- Think about a result that you get, but don't desire. Ask yourself about the different behaviors or habits of yours that led to this result.
- Write about the said behavior or habit in detail.
- Write about the exact opposite of the one you identified in the previous step.
- Write down the good habit or behavior on another sheet of paper.
- You can either shred the paper with the bad habits or burn it. This is a symbolic gesture of eliminating the undesirable habit from your mind.
- Look at the good habit paper daily. Read it out loud, and remind yourself. It will act as a catalyst and make it easier to reprogram your mind.

All your thoughts tend to result in self-perpetuating cycles. The way you think directly influences the way you feel and your behavior. If you think you are a loser, you will feel like a loser. Then, you'll change the way you behave to how you think you should be. This in turn, reinforces the belief that you are a loser. Ouch, that does sound a little harsh, doesn't it? Well, it is pretty much the way your brain works.

You might believe you're not good enough to progress in your career. If you have this assumption in your mind, it not only makes you feel discouraged but will effectively stop you from making any effort. If you don't, you will never get ahead in life. It, in turn, will further reinforce your belief that you are not good enough. If you are in a social setting and only want to stand by yourself in a corner. When no one interacts with you because you've put yourself out of the loop, it reinforces your belief that you are socially awkward. If you believe you are socially awkward, then you will start behaving this way.

Once you have decided on this, there are two things you might end up doing. The first being you will probably look for evidence that supports and reinforces the conclusion. The second is you will start discounting anything that is not in alignment with it. For instance, when someone believes they are a failure, and whenever they make a mistake, it is proof that they are not good enough. If they manage to succeed in something, they will not think it is because of their capabilities, and will instead associate success with just getting lucky. In this situation, if you take a moment for self-reflection, you will realize it was talent that made you successful.

What if it is not your lack of talent or skills that are holding you back in life? What if there is a fault in the way you are thinking? What if your paradigms towards life are skewed? What if you are wrong? There are plenty of "what if's" associated with thinking patterns. Keep in mind your thoughts aren't irrefutable, and they don't necessarily have to be the absolute truth. Try challenging yourself.

Spend some time and consider all the different labels you might have given yourself. Perhaps you have assumed you are incompetent, have low self-confidence, or are a bad leader. Remind yourself that these are just some beliefs that you have about yourself. They don't necessarily have to be true unless you start acting like you believe those assumptions. Apart from all the different tips discussed up until now, there are other ways in which you can change your paradigms.

Start by looking for evidence that disproves your beliefs. Instead of concentrating on all the instances or incidents where your beliefs were reinforced, look for the ones where they were not reinforced. Acknowledge the fact that there are exceptions to every rule and remind yourself that your beliefs are not necessarily true all the time. You can be an exception to your beliefs only if you wish to, and no one can force you to do this.

Start challenging your beliefs and regularly testing whether they are still true or not. If you believe you are not good enough or are unworthy, try stepping outside your comfort zone and do something you have never tried before. You will learn a lot more about yourself than you thought. If you feel like you don't have any confidence, then why not try talking to a stranger? When you start challenging your expectations and see that you are not limited by what you think you are, life will get easier.

Why Reprogram Your Mind?

A negative attitude can be the hidden cause of trouble in your life. Since your thoughts shape your reality, a negative attitude makes your life seem incredibly bad. Now that you are aware of what your paradigms mean and how to change, we look at the benefits of mind reprogramming.

Acquire More Opportunity

You can start seeing opportunities where you once only saw mistakes or failures. Learning to deal with obstacles, setbacks, mistakes, and failure is important to succeed in life. Remember that every cloud has a silver lining, and all you need to do is look for yours. When you mess up, it is a learning opportunity. By reprogramming your mind to look at errors, obstacles, and setbacks as lessons, it becomes easier to move on. If you continually worry about everything that has gone wrong in your past, you won't see the opportunities available to you right now.

Achieve Higher Self-Esteem

When you not only believe, but also expect good things will happen, you will also start to feel good about yourself. This, in turn, will instill you a special kind of confidence. When you start believing in yourself, and have faith in your skills, your chances of succeeding skyrocket. You will find the underlying courage to take on big feats and accomplish things you never knew were possible, all you needed was a little more faith.

Increase Resilience

When you are stuck in a tough spot, or you feel like nothing is going your way, it is quite easy to sink into self-pity. Self-pity merely festers negativity and sends you on a downward spiral. Challenges mean to test you. Live your life believing in this proverb: "when the going gets tough, the tough get going." It's incredibly challenging to keep going when you always expect the worst. Every setback or obstacle seems impossible to overcome when you have a poor attitude. This also magnifies any problems you face in life. Usually, the first ones to complain and quit are the ones who are followed around by a bad attitude.

Inspire Others

Positivity is contagious. When you are around people who radiate positive energy, you will feel better about yourself. So, if you showcase a positive attitude, you can inspire others to do better in life. When you maintain a positive attitude, all those around you will also feel better. It, in turn, creates an overall vibe of positivity that leads to growth.

Overcome Fear

When negativity is coupled with fear, it is the perfect recipe for getting stuck in a rut. Anxiety can be incredibly paralyzing, and if you don't deal with it properly, you can never hope to attain any goals or ambitions properly. A positive mindset attracts courage. Fear is so powerful and it can easily distort your perception and since this determines your reality, it can harm you in so many ways.

Reduce Stress

We lead extremely hectic, stressful lives to no end, and we certainly don't need any more. A little optimism and positivity can effectively diffuse the most stressful of situations. This small tweak in your mindset is an effective way to prevent and alleviate any stress you experience. If you are worried about your finances, it certainly is a source of immense stress. If you keep stressing yourself out, you cannot come up with a solution. Try to think of ways in which you can improve this situation by coming up with a plan to save more, or cut down on unnecessary spending, as well as think of ways to increase earnings. Try to rationally analyze the situation and look for a solution instead of allowing stress to get the better of you.

Motivate Yourself

Positive expectations are incredible motivators. Is there anything you stand to gain if you maintain an attitude that attracts negativity and always expect failure? Well, the only thing that might happen is this assumption can become a self-fulfilling prophecy and everything will come to a grinding halt. Because if you were expecting a negative outcome, who would you want to continue? Let's assume that you have an important presentation due at work. You might be worried your points are weak and your coworkers may not understand or offer support and instead just give you a hard time or criticize you. When you play it out in your head and assume that the outcome will not be favorably, your motivation to keep working on the task at hand will falter. Remind yourself that you cannot predict the future and instead be prepared for the worst and expect the best.

Clearer Interpretations

The way you interpret events is solely based on your attitude at that moment. For example, if you have a fight with your spouse in the morning, you might automatically assume it's going to be a bad day. So, anything that happens during the day, especially the unfavorable moments, will be associated with the fact that it's already bad. Now, if you start viewing every obstacle like this, you cannot move ahead in life. Personal interpretations of events can significantly influence all your decision-making processes. Apart from that, they can also guide your actions in life. If you misinterpret most of the occurrences in your life, you will end up making the wrong decisions.

Deal With Criticism Better

When negative paradigms riddle you, it becomes increasingly difficult to deal with all types of criticism. How do you react when someone questions you? Do you think about it intently before dismissing, or do you accept it as the ultimate truth? Do you get defensive, or does it bring you down? Do you wonder what you might have done to deserve the harsh words? Any and all of those are options when someone speaks up and is received with doubt or disapproval. However, there is one thing that most of us fail to do. There is one question you must ask yourself whenever you are confronted with tough analysis. Do you see it for what it is and try to improve?

If you view it as an opportunity to better yourself, then it is easier to move past it. If you cannot find the bright side of a critique, it can affect your self-confidence and self-esteem. Nothing in life can bother you unless you allow it to. Fortunately, you have the power to decide these things.

If you notice that you don't respond well to judgment, then it is time to rewire your thinking. No one is perfect, and everyone has different expectations. Because of this, people often criticize each other. Just because someone criticizes you, it doesn't mean what they are saying is true, or you are what they are saying. Start trusting and loving yourself. Apart from that, you must also accept yourself before you make any changes.

Your attitude is a precursor to your chances of succeeding in life. When you genuinely believe that the best is yet to come, it gives you the motivation to keep going. You will keep working until you attain your goals. Apart from that, it reduces your stress, makes you feel better about yourself, and attracts more opportunities into your life. A positive attitude is the best weapon at your disposal. What more? You're the only one that has complete control over it.

CHAPTER 5:

Manipulation is Not Bad

Manipulation is Desirable

anipulation doesn't always have to be negative. Manipulation can be classified based on the intention behind it. The primary goal of using manipulation helps to identify good and bad manipulation. The term manipulation might conjure images of emotional predators and narcissists. The true meaning of this term is subjective. Manipulation can be used to turn negative energy into something more positive.

If you use manipulation to help others, it shouldn't always be considered a bad thing. When manipulation is used to serve selfish needs and hurt others, that is where it gets its bad reputation. Maybe there were instances where you wanted to help someone who needed it but they weren't open to what you had to offer. In this case, you can use manipulation to serve him for his own good. So, any tactic you decide to apply for swaying his opinion is not selfish.

On the surface, manipulative tactics seem dishonest and exploitative. If your actions are guided with positive connotations and good intent, then manipulation doesn't seem so wrong. Even if it starts under the pretenses of deceit, if the aim is to help someone, then the end justifies the means. It cannot be considered black and white; it is somewhere in between.

Let us assume one of your friends has recently ended a toxic relationship. They might experience moments of weakness when they are thinking they want to get back together with the ex. In such a situation, as a responsible friend, it is your duty to advise them so as not to make a bad decision. So, maybe you remind them of the time their ex made them feel they could not be trusted or acted shady. Or if it was ever a question of unfaithfulness during the course of their relationship. Maybe you can suggest the ex may have moved on or has found someone else. Yes, you may be hurting them a little by telling this lie, but the end result justifies the means. If this white lie can prevent your friend from rekindling a bad relationship that will only bring them suffering and pain, then temporary hurt can be justified. It is one of the reasons why manipulation lies in the grey area. So, manipulation can be good, provided it is used for the right purposes.

Some of the words used to describe manipulation include organization, manual, direction, administration, machination, and orchestration. In fact, the Webster dictionary defines manipulation as "to manage or use skillfully" (taken verbatim). Well, there are different ways to look at manipulation and it's meaning does change. For instance, if you were given a piece of clay and were asked to manipulate it into a pot, you wouldn't think twice about molding the clay into something. In this instance, a simple change of paradigm alters the way you perceive manipulation. You can use it to shape your life in a way that brings you closer to your dreams while getting rid of any factors that would prevent you from being positive.

There would have been instances in your life when you were required to dial down on certain negative emotions. At times, it becomes difficult to change these emotions or even forget about them. In such situations, the best course of action is to try and alter them. Some of the greatest leaders the world has ever known, like Mahatma Gandhi, Mother Teresa, or Martin Luther King, were all positive manipulators. They did not try to manipulate others, but they needed to change their energy and negative thinking patterns to be able to release their full potential and inherent positivity. It was an effective way to lead by example. They were essentially exhibiting a way of life that could be available to all, if they were just willing to take a serious look at themselves and change a few things. Whenever you meet someone, you make an impression. If it is positive, then the person's energy will also be positive. This is also a simple act of manipulation.

The art of persuasion and effectively influencing others certainly makes it easier for you to express yourself clearly. When you can do this effectively, your arguments will always seem logical and others are bound to agree with you. As these are not based on opinions but facts. You can start with a specific opinion, but by sharing valid information, it becomes easier to show that the opposition is wrong. When you can convince others to follow your lead, it will do wonders for your self-confidence and self-esteem.

Manipulation comes in handy when you are trying to set personal boundaries for yourself. Take some time for self-introspection and think about your limits. What are you willing to do, and how far are you willing to let something go? When you answer these questions, you will realize your boundaries. At times, all you need to do is say no to implement these boundaries. Personal boundaries are also a sign of self-respect, self-worth, self-confidence, and self-love. Unless you have all these important feelings towards yourself, you cannot make others do what you want them to. For instance, your inability to say no might have encouraged others to exploit you in the past. Let us assume that your co-worker used to keep dumping all his work on you, while he used to leave early. Why could he get away with all this? Perhaps it was because of your inability to stand up for yourself and say no. Once you put your foot down, it becomes easier to concentrate on the things that matter and contribute to your personal growth.

Self-Awareness Is the First Step

Your thoughts and interpretations will change as you develop self-awareness. These changes in your mental state alter emotions, boost your emotional intelligence (EQ), and sense of self, all quintessential for succeeding in life. By becoming self-aware, you can easily understand your true passions emotions, and how your personality can benefit you. You can identify where your emotions and thoughts come from, where they are leading, and then make the required changes. Once you are aware of all this, you can change the direction you wish to take in life.

So, what is self-awareness? Self-awareness is quite personal, and it essentially means having a thorough understanding of one's strengths, values, weaknesses, behaviors, habits, and the reasons for the same. Self-awareness brings with it the power to accept one's flaws or mistakes while focusing on self-improvement. If you wish to take control of your life and create a future you desire while mastering your mind, then self-awareness is the first step. There are plenty of things you cannot control in life. However, the one thing you can control is where you wish to focus your energy, your emotions, personality, and reactions. Once you are self-aware, you can see how your thoughts and emotions guide you. Instead of merely reacting to situations in life, you can rationally respond to them. At times, all you need to do is tweak your response to become successful. The ability to change yourself and the power to influence your outcome comes from changing your thoughts and understanding yourself. It certainly takes plenty of time, effort, and patience to develop self-awareness.

Maintain a Journal

Self-reflection increases your self-awareness. Set some time aside for self-reflection and during this period, look at yourself honestly and objectively. This is one of those things that is easier said than done as the constant pressure to do more with less, and the continuous flow of information can be distracting.

One of the best ways to improve your self-awareness is by keeping a journal. Before you go to sleep at night, spend about twenty minutes writing about your daily experiences. There might have been certain things you were happy and unhappy about or things that made you stop and ponder. Once you put these thoughts, emotions, and feelings in writing, understanding them becomes easier. Be honest and don't try to make it sound better than it was, only you will be reading this.

If something bothers you, write about it. At the moment it may seem like a huge issue but after some time has passed and once it's down on paper, it will seem like a petty thing to get hung up on. It gives you a chance to look at why you react in certain ways and what draws specific feelings out that influence you. When you start taking stock of your emotions, and behaviors, making any desirable changes is attainable.

Mindfulness Meditation

Meditation will help make you more mindful and self-aware. Sitting in a quiet spot, tuning out the noise serves as a tool for self-reflection and clarity while also taking a break from your daily life. These are some specific questions you can think about while meditating, and make a difference in your practice.

- Think of your goals, big and small. What are they?
- Are you consciously working towards them? Why or why not?
- What can you do to attain your goals?
- What are the steps you could be taking to better attain your goals?
- What is preventing you from achieving your goals?
- What are the changes you can make to improve?

The answers might not magically come to you while meditating. However, it certainly clears your mind from the clutter, which prevents you from thinking effectively. While meditating, you might come across a multitude of thought patterns, both good and bad. The idea is not to change your thinking; it is merely to accept your thoughts. If you feel like you are drifting away, concentrate on breathing, and refocus your attention. You don't need to spend hours on this to get a better understanding of yourself. Even meditating for 5 to 15 minutes per day will do a world of good and once you start answering these questions, you will notice your self-awareness improving.

Talk to the People in Your Circle

If you are struggling with understanding yourself, talk to your confidants, and reveal the journey of self-discovery you are on. Listen to your peers, mentors, and close companions for their feedback. Allow them to play the role of a mirror and reflect your traits to you. Ensure these are the people who only want the best for you. Ask them to be critical, objective, open, and honest while giving feedback. Ensure that you create a safe environment where they can share their opinions freely and where you feel comfortable to receive them with an open mind. If any comments or questions surface you don't understand, ask them to explain.

Regardless of what the feedback sounds like, ensure that you aren't defensive. After all, you are the one who asked for outsider insight, so learning to deal with criticism constructively is essential. If you are aware of the areas of your life you wish to change or any specific traits you want to let go of or develop, then talk about it. Tell them they have permission to speak up whenever you display any undesirable traits. For instance, if you have the habit of regularly interrupting others while they are talking, ask your friends to make you aware and stop you gently.

Apart from talking to your friends and loved ones, there is another route is asking for opinions of yourself at your place of work. Obtaining feedback from your colleagues, co-workers, team members, or even manager enables you to grasp your impact on a wider scale. It can also help improve any interpersonal relationships you share at work. Self-awareness is not only good for understanding yourself, but it has a positive effect on other aspects of your life as well. It is not just about hearing what they say about you, but how you analyze it. Look at your main takeaway and reflect. Try to see whether they are in sync with the feedback you have received from close friends who see you in a different light. Here you can discover certain strengths or weaknesses you didn't know you had.

Personality Test

There are plenty of personality and psychometric tests you can take to understand your traits. Some of the best self-awareness tests include the Predictive Index and the Myers-Briggs test. Be as honest and open about yourself as you can while answering questions and remember there are no wrong answers. Don't rush through it like a Buzzfeed quiz, spend a good amount of time on these and let the questions sink in. Never feel compelled to respond to specific traits you don't possess. These results are not absolute but are a great way to get a better understanding of yourself. It will give you the insight you need to improve or change certain traits you possess.

Triggers

A trigger is something that prompts an involuntary, almost like a knee-jerk reaction. Identifying your emotional triggers is not an easy process, but it is very important if you want to understand yourself. For instance, if you feel an urge to binge on sugary foods after spending time with someone, it is an emotional trigger. Think about all the people in your life who trigger an instant and unconscious response in you whether it's good or bad. To cope with this you must understand the people in your life, how they make you feel, and the feelings that trigger your reactions. As long as you aren't reacting irrationally, the chances of making a sound decision is likely.

Set Boundaries

The integrity of your goals and your desire to work towards them can be preserved by setting boundaries. Setting boundaries is important in all aspects of your life - personal as well as professional. Unless you know your limits, you cannot determine what you like and don't like. If you don't have any boundaries, it makes you an easy target for other manipulators. To set your boundaries, you need self-awareness. Think about your goals, priorities, and the things you like. Once you are aware of all this, setting and implementing boundaries becomes easy. It takes courage and strength to accept your limits. However, by recognizing your limits, you will know the steps you must take to improve.

New Experiences

Exploring new things will teach you a lot about yourself. You cannot grow in life unless you step outside your comfort zone. Try doing things you never did before. Any fears associated with the unknown also start fading away when you move away from comfort. When you realize that you can do something, you initially thought you couldn't; it will undoubtedly renew your self-confidence.

It can be difficult to develop the level of introspection required for self-awareness and also disappointing when it doesn't come easily. Being honest with yourself is not always easy, and rationally evaluating your weaknesses, and challenges requires a good amount of self-introspection. Set time aside to carefully analyze the good and bad experiences you have had. Think about the things you are glad happened and the things you wish you could do differently. If you made a mistake, accept it, and work to improve. When you become aware of yourself, you will understand your mindset is all that stands between you and success.

CHAPTER 6:

Rewiring the Mind

The Law of Attraction

Regardless of your religious beliefs, age, sex, or even nationality, all humans are susceptible to the fundamental laws of the universe, including the law of attraction. This law primarily harnesses the power of the mind to materialize your thoughts into reality. Simply put, any idea can transform itself into existence. If you focus on negative thoughts, you will always have a dark cloud following you. If you start focusing on what you want to achieve and stay positive, your chances increase.

The law of attraction essentially states that whatever you think and hold in your mind's eye can be achieved, provided you take the required action and stick to a plan that enables you to attain them. Not a lot of people are aware of the true impact this has on their lives. Regardless of whether we do it knowingly, we act as magnets sending out our emotions and whatever goes along with them, and attract this same energy back. Sadly, many of us are still blind to the true potential that lies within so it becomes quite easy to leave things unchecked. You might end up sending out negative feelings as a way you think expels it, but in turn, attract more of the unwanted emotion. Since your thoughts guide your actions, these thinking patterns result in more negativity entering in your life.

What goes up must come down, that is the basic principle of gravity. What happens when you throw a ball into the air? It doesn't go to the next town over, it comes back directly to you, depending on your aim. Newton's third law of motion states that every action has an equal and opposite reaction. So, if you throw a ball at a wall with some force, the ball will bounce back with the same intensity. Now, instead of a physical object, think about the energy, thoughts, and actions, you are putting outward into the universe. If they are riddled with skepticism, doubt or fear, you are merely attracting more of this negativity into your life.

Buddha first taught the law of attraction hundreds of years ago. It is said he wanted every human to know that what we have become is the product of our thoughts - a belief deeply synonymous with this philosophy. When this concept started spreading in Western culture, a new term came into popularity, karma. Do you remember the saying, "you reap what you sow?" Over the centuries, it has become a common belief that what you give out to the world is the return you can expect in the end.

The power of thinking and the presence of universal energy is described in all religious scriptures. Proverbs 23:7 states, "As a man thinketh in his heart, so is he."

The universe will respond enthusiastically to all energy vibrations you send out. It doesn't discriminate between the vibrations, it merely responds. Whatever you think or feel at any given moment is essentially your request to the universe, asking for more. Since your energy vibrations attract the energy of the same frequency back into your life, ensure that you send out the energy you desire. There are three simple steps you must follow while using the law of attraction, and they are as follows.

Step #1: Ask
You send out requests not just to your subconscious, but also the universe in the form of your thoughts. Everything that you think, pay attention to, read, and say out loud is a request. Sadly, most of this attention is oblivious and a reaction to something. The law of attraction states that you will attract into your life whatever you dedicate your focus to. Start being more deliberate with your thoughts, actions, and emotions by deciding what you want in the present day. Maybe you want to change your career, move to a new city, finally recover from an illness, or save more money. Concentrate on how you will feel once you achieve it, picture how your life will look, and who will be next to you. Try to steer your conversations in this direction and concentrate on what you want.

Step #2: Believe
The second step is to believe that you will get what you want and act on it. Start believing that your future rests in the hands of a higher power. It is about believing with pure convection that whatever you want will come to you but it won't always be so easy to maintain this attitude. Most of us have limiting

beliefs that prevent us from living our life to the fullest or unlocking true potential. If this applies to you, the first step is to change your limiting beliefs. Let go of any self-limiting beliefs and assumptions you have and, instead, replace them with more desirable thoughts. Once you believe that you can get what you want, the second step is to take action.

Step #3: Receive

If you want to receive whatever you are intending, you must be a vibrational match for the kind of energy you wish to attract into your life. Start showing and feeling those emotions as if you have already reached your goals. Concentrate on thinking and living your life, focusing on all the things you desire. Instead of allowing the troubles of daily life to hold you down, concentrate on the good you desire. Visualize the kind of life you wish to lead or the things you want, and concentrate on these positive feelings. You will learn more about visualizations in the subsequent sections.

What Is a Negative Paradigm?

Nothing is inherently good or bad; the way you think makes it so. You might have studied hard for an exam, but before you enter the exam hall, you might wonder, "What if I fail?" Perhaps you hesitate to ask someone out on a date because you are afraid of rejection. You might feel anxious about an important presentation because you fear that no one will agree or understand. Everyone has been in these situations at one point or another in their life, where we second-guess ourselves or become overwhelmed with pessimism. We will go so far as to start believing our baseless thoughts. These kinds of thoughts can lead to anxiety, or even depression if left unchecked.

Whenever a new opportunity is available, what are your first thoughts? Maybe excitement or a sense of determination will arise. But after some time do you think about missing the mark and disappointing anyone connected to it? If so, that is a clear sign of a negative paradigm existing in your mind. These thoughts make us believe that the world is a dark and scary place, unyielding and meant to test you, even when that is not the case. Any thought patterns based on disqualifying the positive while exaggerating the negatives is bad. By making a mountain out of a molehill, you are overestimating the negative attributes, while minimizing any positivity associated with the many complicated situations that happen in life requiring more than one emotion to comprehend. The glass is either half empty or half full, and it depends on you to decide which. It is important to understand what negative thoughts mean, and recognize these patterns if you wish to rewire your brain. Since these thoughts shape your reality, learn to control them.

How to Recognize Negative Patterns

You cannot change something if you don't know what it is exactly. Negative thinking reduces the chances of success in life and increases the risk of various mental health problems that can affect your physical state. If your mind is conditioned to only look at the negative aspects of your life, you will not understand true happiness even if it is staring right at you. A simple acronym you can use to discern negative thought patterns is BLUE and explained in detail below.

Blaming Oneself

If you make a mistake or hurt someone, it is important to take responsibility for it. However, you cannot blame yourself for everything that goes wrong in life. Excessive self-blame is detrimental to growth and even happiness to some extent. If you constantly tell yourself, "it is all my fault," or "I've ruined everything" then it is highly unlikely you will be able to see the good in any situation. If you make a mistake, learn from it, make amends, and move on. Excessive indulgence in self-blame is not going to do you any good. In fact, it will bring your moral down and prevent you from taking any action.

Look for the Bad News

If you actively look for bad news in every situation, you cannot see any good whatsoever. If five good things and one bad thing happened to you on a given day, what will you concentrate on? Someone with positive thinking will focus on the good and not the bad. If your paradigm toward life is generally negative, then you cannot relish the good things and will get bogged down by the one bad thing. If you keep dwelling on negativity, you will get stuck in a darkened, miserable place. In such situations, take a step back and try to look at your life from a realistic perspective. Life isn't always bad, and neither is it always good. It is a mix of both these aspects that makes it worth living. Celebrate all the good things that happen to you instead of worrying about the one thing that didn't.

Unhappy Predictions

No one can predict the future. The future can be good or bad. Things can go your way, or the worst might come true. If you have no idea what will happen tomorrow, predicting doom and gloom will only bring you down today. Remember, the law of attraction? The kind of energy you think about and give out is the kind of energy you will receive. So, if you imagine that you will end up embarrassing yourself in front of your colleagues or tell yourself you will never get the promotion you want, this kind of negative thinking might transform into a self-fulfilling prophecy. Stop making unhappy predictions about the future. Instead, try to do your best today and rest easy, knowing that the universe always rewards those who do their best.

Exaggeration of the Negative

If you keep telling yourself your job interview was an utter disaster, or are convinced that everything about your life is terrible; it leads you down on a downward spiral of self-pity, negativity, and everything undesirable. The more negative thoughts you harbor, the worse you will feel. The worse you feel, the less likely it is that you will be able to take any positive action in life. So, stop sabotaging your life and happiness by giving into negative thinking.

Patterns to Avoid

Overthinking

When you constantly go over the same situations in your mind, trying to imagine the various outcomes of what can happen in the future you end up only concentrating on the things that can go wrong. The main problem with overthinking is that in your bid to try and control, it becomes unmanageable. You can't predict the future.

For instance, if you are in a relationship, you cannot successfully predict the outcome of the pairing or what your future together will look like. Things change, problems surface, all you can do is try your best to keep your relationship alive, and healthy making sure you are happy and you are doing your best to make the other person happy. Overthinking can take the joy away from any huge life changes like promotions, marriage, buying a house, or moving to a new city. It can make you averse to taking risks or even scared to act.

If all of your time is spent thinking, instead of doing, how will you ever know how your life was supposed to pan out? This rumination over trivial details causes unnecessary stress and can keep you from making a decision leaving you in a constant state of limbo. Whenever you feel like you are thinking a little too much about one choice, give yourself a deadline. In fact, if it helps, give yourself a deadline for every decision. Allow yourself to think about only a couple of alternatives and stop being so hard on yourself. It is okay to make a mistake or pick wrong. It's never too late to fix your mistakes, provided you are willing to act. Unless you try, you will never know.

Negative Reflection

Reflection will give you better insight into the things you have said or done in your past. but it can become problematic when it starts becoming excessive. If you keep going over your past, you will get stuck there in a rut comparable to quicksand. The more you try to wiggle out, the deeper you sink, and the harder it is to get out. Negative reflection is similar to overthinking in a lot of ways but with overthinking, you end up spending a lot of time dwelling about a situation, the possible outcomes, and things you may have done wrong or can go wrong. When it comes to negative reflection, your perception of a situation itself is cloaked in negativity.

If you have problems staying present, it will make enjoying life that much more difficult. This kind of dwelling can make you extremely anxious as you worry about the negative outcomes instead of concentrating on the good in life. If you ever feel lonely, don't start thinking that you will be lonely forever, never meet, your soulmate, never have a family, or lose all your friends. Negative thinking of this sort can also make you feel incredibly depressed. Start focusing on how bad you feel, the reasons for the same, the mistakes you made that led to the situation, and how things can worsen. Even before you start, you have already imagined the worst. Since you focus only on the negatives that come out of the situation, your inner motivation goes away.

The simplest way to get over this kind of negative reflection is by paying attention to when these thoughts crop up in your mind, whenever you notice you can't shake the thought of something undesirable, take a break. By merely removing yourself from one location and putting yourself somewhere else can help. If you are stuck at work and start ruminating over unnecessary things, then take a break and go for a walk. If you feel lonely, call up a friend and talk about it for a while.

Cynical Hostility

Any thoughts or reactions stemming from the general anger or mistrust of others is known as cynical hostility. If you constantly think of those around you as a threat, it makes it impossible to trust anyone. You assume they are unreliable, have ulterior motives, take you for a fool, or are trying to deceive you. When you default to this when meeting someone new, you cannot expect to form any healthy or lasting relationships. I'm not saying naïvete is the answer or to trust everyone without question but being extremely pessimistic of those around you is not the way.

For instance, what will you think when you are stuck in traffic? If you think that all the drivers ahead of you are deliberately driving slowly, it can make you easily frustrated and angry. Instead, if you merely acknowledge the fact that you are stuck in a traffic jam, and it isn't deliberate, you can avoid feeling frustrated.

So, how can you change this pattern of thinking? The first step is to prevent yourself from jumping to conclusions. Give yourself a while before you judge anyone or anything. Not everyone around you has toxic or evil intentions. Look for evidence and look at it rationally before you draw any conclusions.

How to Replace Negative Patterns

Now that you know how to identify negative thought patterns, it's time to get rid of them and make space for those that serve you. You know that the way you view the world primarily depends on your attitude and affects everything from your career to your personal life and health. And thanks to the law of attraction, negative attracts negative. The good news now is you can slowly but surely, train your mind to replace negative thought patterns with more positive ones and here's how.

Make Time for You in the Morning

Your mind gets a fresh start in the morning. If your usual morning routine consists of replying to emails or spending time on social media, instead try to include certain positive and constructive activities to your normal routine. Take this time to focus and meditate on the kind of person you wish to be and the life you want to lead.

Start your day instead with positive affirmations. When you wake up in the morning and open your eyes, express your gratitude for the new day you have been granted. Every new day allows you to start afresh. Make a list of daily words you can use, such as "I love my job and the people I work with," "I am changing my life for the better," or "I am working towards my dreams daily."

The simplest way to prevent negativity from getting hold of you is by not leaving any room in your mind for it to creep in. If you give your mind something positive to dwell on, you will not have the time for anything else. These affirmations help recondition and reprogram your subconscious mind. When you think a specific thought frequently, you start believing it. So, start leveraging the power of positive affirmations to assure positivity into your life. Also consider writing a list of things you want to accomplish for the day. Focus on your goals, usher some positivity into your life little by little.

Be Your Own Cheerleader

It is quite easy to be negative about oneself. In fact, most of us are extremely critical of our lives, the things we do, the decisions we make, and so on. You cannot let go of this habit unless you start to love yourself. Learn to be your personal motivator, cheerleader, and coach. Be your best friend. Your source of happiness or positivity doesn't necessarily have to stem from outside, and it comes from within. Here are some simple steps you can follow to let go of certain negative self-talk.If there is a negative thought in your mind, release it. The first step is to write, talk, or express the negative thoughts to yourself and not delve on it. You get three minutes to feel bad for yourself and indulge in self-criticism. Once the time's up, it is time to let go. The second step is to keep track of your thought patterns. Learn to identify whenever negative thoughts pop into your mind. It is where self-awareness comes into the picture so follow the steps discussed about self-awareness in previous sections to do this. The third step is to start reframing it. Once you are aware of your reasons for all the criticism, consider the advice you would give a loved one if she were in the same situation. If your best friend were stuck in a tough spot, how would you behave? Now, it is time to show the same compassion and love towards yourself.

Feel Love and Gratuity

Now, it is time to make a little conscious effort to find all the things you enjoy and appreciate in life. Instead of using your mental energy to fight negative thoughts, seek better feelings. A powerful way to do this is by talking about the things you love, cherish, appreciate, and enjoy in life. It doesn't have to be anything significant. It could be something as simple as your morning cup of coffee. If you take a moment and think about it, there will be plenty of things in your life you can be grateful for like a supportive partner and family members to good friends, a job you love, or maybe even the house you live in. Look for the little joys in life and focus on the good. When you keep a positive mindset as you go about your day, positivity will find you. Spend at least five minutes daily to think about all the things you are truly grateful for. Once you ignore the previous patterns, your mind will concentrate on new ones.

Replace Bad with Good

You cannot overcome your negative thought patterns unless you start replacing them. Negative thought patterns are often stuck in your neural pathway, and you cannot eliminate this pathway, but you can certainly tweak it. There are four simple steps you must follow to replace any negative thought patterns.

The first step is to pinpoint where the negative thought patterns originate. There are different instances that will trigger them. The second step is to acknowledge what you wish to change. So, even if it is extremely negative, you must accept it because it is the only way to dismiss it. The third step is to rephrase the thought. If you think, "I can't do this," change it to "I might not be able to do it right now." By merely changing the way you think, you can affect the way you feel about specific things in your life. The fourth step is to select a different behavior that helps you attain your goals. If you feel overwhelmed whenever you need to do something new, all you need to do is start with the first step. Once you do this, it gives you the momentum to keep going.

Make Time for Negative Thoughts

It might seem counter-productive to set time aside for thinking negative thoughts but by doing this, you ensure that you don't become distracted by them throughout the day so you stay productive. Whenever a negative thought pops into your mind during the day, make a note of it and return to it during the allotted time frame you set. During this time feel free to exercise critical thinking by asking yourself the tough questions.

- Do these negative thought patterns help me in any way? Do I stand to gain anything from them?
- Will I lose anything if I change these negative thought patterns? Are there any costs involved?
- Are there any benefits I stand to gain by changing these thought patterns?
- What other things or events in my past that led me to form these beliefs?
- Once you answer these questions, it becomes easier to understand your thought patterns and change them.

Write it Out

At times, all you need to do to let go of a pesky thought is express it and writing is a fantastic way to do that. Once you make a note of it, you are purging it from your system. The minute the words are visible on paper, the situation becomes clear. Often, the biggest obstacles are manageable when broken down into pieces, and being able to see it manifested on paper or a screen is how you start. Maybe you are stuck in a situation that seems impossible to deal with. Instead of letting it swirl around inside your head with no boundaries this form of self-expression not only improves your sense of clarity but can enable you to come up with an impressive array of solutions.

Start a New Habit

By merely changing the way you look at your plan to deal with negative thought patterns, you can make progress. Instead of thinking about overcoming, think about establishing new habits. Every thought pattern in your mind is like a different road. If you are stuck on one path or one thought all the time, it is like traveling down the same road. So, if it is not used as much it will slowly move out of your mind and no longer be an option. It is believed that it takes about a month to break or form a new habit. If you are trying to replace your existing thought patterns, changing them isn't easy, but it is doable. Instead of thinking you aren't good enough or you cannot do something, try to think of all the things you are good at. Whenever you feel like you cannot achieve something, break it down into smaller objectives and accomplish them slowly. Remind yourself of all your accomplishments and it gives you the motivation to keep going.

Channel Your Thoughts

Negative thoughts can creep up quite easily, and negative thought patterns are the easiest ones to develop. If you are at the conscious effort, they can quickly get a hold of you. Instead of channeling your mental energy, thinking about these negative thoughts, channel it towards something you are excited about. You are merely changing the way your mental energy flows and directing it towards something better in life. For instance, whenever you are thinking about a negative thought, gather your mental energy, and refocus it on a thought that you are excited about. If you are worried that you will not be able to complete a project, then think about a project you love working on. You are merely distracting yourself from dwelling on the negativity, by concentrating on the positive aspects of your life.

Exercise

Another way to put a stop to negative thoughts is through movement. Getting your heart rate up, breaking a sweat, any type of physical exertion will put you in a completely different state of mind that produces the feel-good hormones your body craves. Start exercising daily or spend time engaging in a physical activity you enjoy. You don't need to workout at the gym, you can walk through the park, run in your favorite neighborhood, or go swimming. Turn your home into a dance studio and dance your heart out to your best playlist. Exercise is not just good for your physical health but improves your mental well-being.

Skills for Manipulation

Unless you can express your thoughts and opinions clearly and effectively, you will not give anyone a reason to listen. It is one of the four skills to become a master manipulator. Perhaps the simplest way to improve is to start reading. Read as much as you can, gather information, improve your vocabulary, and never stop learning. Information will always be your best resource, and if you use it wisely, you can achieve anything. Try to read about different topics, stay current on world events, and avoid restricting yourself to a specific category. This enables you to connect with people from all walks of life, and so you'll always have something to say.

The way others feel about you is essentially influenced by the way you talk and present yourself. Pay attention to the way you speak along with your body language. Practice your speaking skills by standing in front of the mirror. You can also record yourself and replay the recordings to notice how you look while speaking. Maybe you have a nervous twitch or movements you were unaware of before. Learn to regulate the tone and pitch of your voice. This will help drive the message home. If you come across as sarcastic or harsh, you will not effectively reach your audience. Modulate and play with your voice. Your voice, along with the pitch, enables you to engage your listeners and grab their attention effectively. Whenever you speak, make sure it is with vitality and ensure that it is loud and clear.

The way you present yourself creates a specific impression in your target's mind. Self-presentation speaks volumes as you can use your looks to your advantage if you know how. When it comes to physical appearance, genetics don't really matter. Following a good routine of self-care and grooming contribute to your overall appearance. Maintaining basic hygiene, wearing a good scent, and dressing smartly make you seem more confident. Ensure that the clothes you wear suit your body type and accentuate your best features. Well-fitted clothes can instantly improve appearance. When you start dressing better, you will feel better about yourself. When you seem confident it triggers the same response from others. First impressions last, so ensure that you make it a good one every time.

Learn as much about human behavior and psychology as you can. You might have to do your own research on this to be effective. We have gone through much of the basics in this book, but there is always more to learn. It is up to you to decide if it's worth it. All of the techniques discussed in this chapter are not only simple to follow but practical too. Commit to improving yourself, and you can see a positive change within no time. It takes repetition, consistency, time, effort, and patience to rewire your mind. If you are willing to make this commitment, then the results will reflect it.

Importance of Visualization and Repetition

The process of thinking is an amalgamation of mental images, sentences, sensations, and words. Thoughts are like visitors that occasionally drop by to say hello. However, some persist for longer. The longer an idea stays in your mind, the more power it gathers. The more power it has, the greater the influence it will have over your life. Most people struggle with letting go of thoughts associated with unhappiness, worry, anger, or fear. All this is because of the negative internal dialogue that continues.

All your inner conversations tend to influence your subconscious. Therefore, it is quintessential you pay attention to what you feed your subconscious. Words, as well as thoughts, become stronger because of repetition. When you repeat them enough, they start sinking into your subconscious mind, and it, in turn, affects your behavior, actions, along with your reactions.

The subconscious mind considers your thoughts as an expression or description of a real situation so it actively tries to align your thoughts with what it thinks is reality. Since it cannot distinguish between what is good or bad, it doesn't discriminate between your thoughts. If your thoughts are deeply rooted, then your actions are guided by your subconscious. Therefore, negative thoughts = negatively influenced actions.

When you keep doing something over and over again, you eventually form a habit. Once a habit is formed, it will influence the way you act depending on the scenario. Likewise, if you think negative thoughts over and over again, they become a part of your regular mindset. This is how the power of repetition can be used for breaking free of negative thought patterns and cultivating good ones. For instance, if you want to learn to say no, then start by saying no to small things. This is the simplest way to stand up for yourself. For instance, if you don't feel like drinking, but your friend is forcing you to drink, you can say no. You don't have to do something merely because you are worried about how others might think about you. You are not responsible for their emotions or ideas. The only person you are responsible for is you.

Another simple technique you can use to reprogram your mind is visualization. Visualization is having a clear picture in your mind of what you desire as a permanent fixture. For instance, if you want to learn to say no, then start visualizing how you would feel and how different your life would be if you were good at saying no. Try to make your visualization clear and include every minute detail. By doing this, you are painting a mental picture of all the benefits you stand to gain by becoming more confident in life. This message becomes embedded in your subconscious mind. Think about all the situations you could have avoided or the things you could have achieved had you said no.

Once you have the visualization in place, start living your life as if you have already attained your goals. Whenever you have to make a decision, ask yourself, what would a self-confident person do? If you are trying to be like someone you idolize, then ask yourself, what would your idol do in such a situation? Visualization is not about putting on a facade of pretending to be someone you are not. Instead, it is about living your life the way you wish you did. It is about breaking free of any self-inflicted limiting beliefs that prevent you from excelling in life.

Reprogramming your brain is a major change, and you cannot make it unless you put in consistent effort. This effort takes dedication, motivation, time, and patience. If you feel like you're not making any progress, then it is time to take a break and that's OK. Keep in mind that every function has a limit. If it feels like it is becoming a little too much, then it probably is. Your brain is not a tireless machine, and neither are you. Take as many breaks as you need, and don't be in a hurry.

So, how do you know when you have attained your goal? How do you know if you have successfully rewired your brain? Well, there is no scientific formula you can use to ascertain the answer to this question. It all depends on your experiences and what you think. If you notice that you seem more confident than before, then you have accomplished something. If you have become more aware of your thoughts, emotions, and understand why you feel the way you feel, it is also a sign of progress. Apart from that, you can always ask for feedback from others. You can talk to your close friends and ask them to evaluate any progress they have seen in you lately. You don't have to tell them exactly what you are trying to do, but find out if they have noticed any changes in you.

CPSIA information can be obtained
at www.ICGtesting.com
Printed in the USA
BVHW042149050521
606340BV00014B/1567